To categorize Rich Boucher's poetry as surreal, brutalist, confessional, dystopian, absurdist, etc. would by no means be inaccurate, but it would certainly be banal. I would prefer to say that he has mastered his native tongue to the extent that he can subvert English and its rules of grammar and syntax to his every poetic purpose, and that he is a dogged and savage critic of the deranged commercialism that menaces our very civilization – but although he frequently finds himself engulfed by the vile smoke of corporatist delusion, he can still hold up an undefiled vision of the joy – and the redemption – that beauty and love may bring to even the most warped and jaded victims of our horrid version of "the great society".

> Arabella Bianco, Board member of the Delaware Literary Connection (Retired), long-time contributor to Delaware's Dreamstreets Magazine, and authoress of "*Disappearances of the Hour Hand*" and "*Sappho's Midnight Garden Party*"

With Rich Boucher you may start out on Earth but end up somewhere in outer space wondering how you're going to get home. It's like Dali was born as Magritte and Magritte was born as Dali and they wake up naked in America wondering what the heck do we do now. In other words, prepare to be transported God knows where or wherever Rich puts you. Some poems are right here in the nitty gritty of home and speak straight from the heart, but most are little fairy tales with no fairy and a cutoff tale, or a totally regrown tail. Prose poem or poem texts speak in Rich Boucherese and watch out, you will laugh unaccountably or simply wonder what planet you're on, but then, with a bump, realize you are right here in America listening to an American voice telling you how it really is. These are texts for serious storytelling that turn out to be funny, in fact, a surprised guffaw followed by a weird embarrassment - "did I laugh at that?" That you did and you will again if Rich takes the floor.

Larry Goodell, Duende Press, Placitas, New Mexico

Surprise! What you hold in your hands is, quite simply, surprise manifest. This collection of poetry by Rich Boucher sparkles with an intelligence at work and at play. On almost any page, you'll be surprised, in awe that one person can have these thoughts and put this combination of words down. It makes for fascinating and fun reading and you, surely, will not want to put it down. Put it next to your bed or in your bathroom bookshelf because this is not a collection to gather dust or sit forgotten on a shelf, this is a book that calls out and says, simply, "Read me!"

> Don McIver, editor of The Bigger Boat: the Unlikely Success of the ABQ Slam Scene, winner of a Basic Human Needs award, radio producer, and performer who proudly calls Albuquerque home.

This is an extraordinarily exciting, Europeanly enticing creation by Albuquerque's premier poet of humor and randomly kinky associative thinking. Rich Boucher's first full-length book is *more than well worth the 40+ year wait!* I wonder in amazement – where does he GET this stuff? On many pages at least three out-loud guffaws grab your funny bone. On others you may be angered, or your heart moved to tears. I am so proud when I see Rich wearing the M. C. Escher tie I loaned to him! Follow poet Boucher along this path of flambunctious feelings and down a rabbit hole of wryly twisted mind and language! A magnificently entertaining book … and also the candy is exquisitely delicious!

> Billy Brown, PhD, poet, poetry publisher and 10-year host of the Fixed and Free poetry readings in Albuquerque, NM.

All of this Candy Belongs to Me

Hey John Mocker!

Thank you for ALL
of your words & your
encouragement! I hope
you like the words!

— Rich Boucher

.

All of This Candy Belongs to Me

Rich Boucher

Cover photo: Leann Denman
Photo Cover Concept and Editing: Rich Boucher
Cover design: Denise Weaver Ross
"Refrigerator" illustration by Kurt Dolber
"Big Sky" illustration by Byron Andrews

ISBN 9781729091234

Acknowledgements

The author would like to acknowledge the following publications
in which these poems first appeared:

Adobe Walls, After the Pause, antinarrative journal, Apeiron Review, Ballard Street Poetry Journal, Bending Genres, Boston Poetry Magazine, Brawler, Broadkill Review, Carnival, Catching Calliope, Citizens for Decent Literature, Crack the Spine, Cultural Weekly, Damfino Press, Dead Snakes, Drunk Monkeys, Eunoia Review, Fixed and Free Poetry Anthology, Foliate Oak, FreezeRay, Gargoyle, Hypertext, In Between Hangovers, Lotus-Eater, Malpais Review, Manzano Mountain Review, Menacing Hedge, Minute Magazine, Missive, MockingHeart Review, Mo' Joe: The Anthology, MoonPark Review, Neon, 99 Poems for the 99 percent, Oddball Magazine, penwheel lit, Philosophical Idiot, Poydras Review, Quarter After, Red Fez, Rhysling Anthology, River and South Review, Runcible Spoon, Soft Cartel, Survival: A Poets Speak Anthology, The Bicycle Review, The Gap Toothed Madness, The Lake, The Mas Tequila Review, The Rag, The Subterranean Quarterly, The Yellow Ham, This Is Poetry, Tinderbox Poetry Journal, Visceral Uterus, Walls: A Poets Speak Anthology, Word Machine, Yellow Chair Review

In our house
we have a refrigerator.
It freezes our food cold.
Stone cold.

Table of Contents

III.   Black Licorice Twist

IV.   White Chocolate

V.   Cinnamon Imperial

Forward

What can I say about my friend Rich Boucher? I suppose the first thing that must be said is that Rich is a poet. While that would seem a pretty obvious and unnecessary thing to say in the forward of a book of poetry, it's worth thinking about for a moment. To choose poetry as one's vocation is one thing, but there are still a lot of other things that most of us need to do just to survive in this world: work needs to be done, life needs to be lived and food needs to be put on the table. Despite having all of these "distractions" in his life I believe that the title of poet still best describes and suits Rich. In fact I'd even go so far as to say that the title defines him at this point.

Rich has been working on his chosen craft for more than thirty years now. Over the past four decades he has been writing and performing his works. In addition to reading at open mic nights and featured shows he has also been a member of several poetry slam teams and his work has been published in many print and online journals. In the early days he even self-published a number of journals and chapbooks of his own. Rich has continued to hone his craft throughout all of these years and he has a distinctive style and voice in his writing. In his poetry you will find humor, satire, personal loss, pop culture references, political commentary, personal reflection and a lot of his own life experiences all mixed together and put into a poetic format. While this is indeed a book of poetry, it is also in many ways a work of nonfiction. It can almost be looked at as an autobiography if you read close enough and put all the pieces together. This book is a pretty comprehensive collection of Rich's works from his earliest interest in poetry right up to recently written poems. In fact the first poem you will read is a short piece about a refrigerator that he wrote in an English class in high school. This piece can arguably be considered his very FIRST poem, and a major part of the impetus for him choosing the path of poetry as a means of expressing himself. The reaction he got from reading that poem in class from his teacher and fellow students really spoke to him about the power of the pen and stayed with him long after the school bell rang.

While honored, I'm also a bit surprised that Rich would choose me to write the forward to something as important to him as <u>All of This Candy Belongs to Me</u>. I am not a poet. I don't even claim to know much about poetry. And in fact I'm not really even a writer at all (unless you consider blogging to be writing)! But what I do have is a long history with Rich. I probably know him as well as anyone. We have been best friends for most of our lives. In fact we are lucky enough to be part of a four-member group of best friends who have been extremely close since elementary school. Time and distance have separated us over the years, but whenever we get a chance to get together (either in person, online or over the phone) we can always pick right up where we left off in our mutual friendships like we were never apart. It's a rare thing that we all know we are very fortunate to have. I think this is the reason Rich asked me to write this forward. He wanted someone who knew him as well as anyone possibly could. And he also wanted to make sure his closest friends were involved in a project that is as close to his heart as this book is. In addition to my forward the book also features illustrations from our other two "besties", Kurt Dolber and Byron Andrews.

Knowing Rich for so long means that I've been there for many important moments in his life. I was there when he read that very first poem about his refrigerator in high school that was mentioned above. I was there when he decided that writing poetry was going to be his "thing". When he shared that with me I have to admit now that my first thought was that it would prove to be a passing phase. How wrong I was on that one! I was there when he really started to grow as a poet in college--both through the scholarly pursuit of knowledge and via the more social aspects of college life. I was there when he asked me to accompany him on his first-ever open mic night experience at the Worcester Artists Group (WAG). It's amazing to recall how nervous and uncertain he was that night, compared to the confident and polished performer he has become over the years. I was also there when he lost each of his parents at too-young an age--experiences that caused him to question many of his beliefs and even his faith in religion. All of his life experiences from childhood and adulthood, both the good and bad, and even some of his dreams (both literal and figurative), have been used in his poetry in some way. You will see all of it in many different forms on the pages that follow.

Since I do have such a long history with Rich I would like to take this opportunity to close out my introduction to him and his book by sharing my earliest memory of him. While kind of random, this odd little story somehow manages to speak volumes about who he was back then, who he is now and who he will continue to be for the rest of his life.

Rich moved to our small town while we were in fourth grade. He wasn't able to start at the beginning of the school year, so his introduction during the year was even more of a standout event. I recall being in class and sitting in about as nondescript a seat as one could--kind of in the middle-left part of the classroom. This class was taught by a teacher who just happened to be the vice-principal. That meant that he was also the chief disciplinarian of the school. And he fit that part well: he was tall, deep-voiced and cast an imposing figure. Rich showed up one day as a new student. I don't recall him being introduced, but I do remember his shock of red hair (a trait that would later lead to the longstanding nickname "Beacon" among our group of friends). He sat right in the center in the front row of the classroom. I've always assumed that he was assigned this seat as a new student and he didn't pick it himself (though I can't say this with any authority). Now, if I were to find myself in that kind of position on my first day at a new school where I didn't know anyone, I'm pretty sure that I would try to be as quiet and unobtrusive as possible. But Rich wasn't me. He sat right up there in the front of the class and put his R2-D2 radio on his desk. I also don't have much of a memory of that radio (for reasons that will become clear very soon), but I do recall it being a VERY cool thing for a kid to have, especially at that point in the late-1970s when the original release of "Star Wars" was all the rage. It was certainly something that would act as a good icebreaker while trying to connect with a school full of people who were completely new to you. But Rich didn't wait until recess or after school to show off his cool toy. Instead, right in the middle of class he decided to turn it on! Yes, while our teacher/vice-principal was in the middle of teaching the day's lesson Rich decided it was a good time to turn his R2-D2 radio on!

I don't really recall what happened next. In my hazy recollection there was some sort of commotion at the front of the class and then Rich didn't seem to be there anymore. The rest of the day passed by normally. The next day Rich was once again in the classroom. He was once again sitting in the middle of the front row. He once again had his R2-D2 radio. But there was one major difference. On this day R2-D2 wasn't sitting proudly on his desk for all to see. On this day the poor little droid was smashed to bits and he was carrying the pieces in a plastic bag. What had happened between that first and second day at the new school? I don't really know for sure, but it was all part of my introduction to Rich. It was something that I eventually came to realize was a part of what Rich was all about. And it was just one of the many, many events and experiences of Rich's life that would all become woven into the fabric of the poems that you will find in this book. In the end, All of This Candy Belongs to Me IS Rich Boucher.

Glen Schultzberg

On a particular Tuesday night, a poet who disliked me and who HATED the slam, came in just as I was making introductory and opening remarks on the microphone and he laid that very sheet you see in the photo down on the floor, in front of the microphone stand base as I spoke. It was his way of peeing in my sandbox and making his own "statement" about what I was doing to the scene back in Delaware.

For Leann,
who brings such sweet light
into this life I know

I.
Cotton Candy Forever

Your Monster Has Never Left You

The monster you grew up with,
he has loved you ever since
your first scream in the bedroom.

He hasn't changed one bit
now that you've become an adult
with a white home of your own,

which includes a closet for him
within your silent night bedroom
where you can still conjure his face.

Do you know that your monster
has always been by your side,
all through your time in college

and through your marriage
and divorce and children
and your troubles at your job?

All that you ever need to do,
if you need a shoulder to cry on,
is admit that he is there,
 there in your closet, loving you,
 waiting for you.

Bundle of Joy

Everyone, mostly the women but a few men, too, flocked around the new mother when she came back to visit the office on Friday. It was a touching and beautiful and touching scene that touched everyone involved in a beautifully touching way. There was a lot of touching, and the smell of baby lotion mixed with the smell of office and copier toner clouded the room and then a bunch of cherubs overhead vibrated with glee so hard their heads blasted apart. There was so much emotion about the new baby that everyone was touching each other. So much oohing and cooing commotioning right there in the middle of the Accounting Department. Jackie wanted to show her baby off at least once before heading back home to enjoy what little remained of her maternity leave. She pulled the downy pink blanket to the side to show off her baby gun. Infant weapon. Just a few weeks old. It was adorable and everyone energetically agreed upon that until they came. Lovable. Jet-black. Blued steel. Hot cold. Nine-millimeter. The baby gun made a weak little sleeping sound as Jackie handed it off to Pauline, who was so anxious to hold it her nipples leaped forward through her blouse and made loud munching noises. The little baby gun appeared almost to be smiling in its slumber. So precious.

The Elderly Hulk

I didn't remember that the episode was called *"The First"*, or maybe I never knew it was called that. I was so young, young like a flower with a strange name in a summer home, home being sort of like a place where I could grow and change, change being a time we live through whether we want to or not. I was only thirteen years old, and I wasn't even thirteen for very long at all, perhaps a year at the most. It's difficult to say how long a person can be thirteen for. Memories are things very strange: they can be affected by trauma, a person's body height and mass, and the mouth consumption of sugar, among four other things that can affect human memory. The episode's title makes sense *now* of course; Bill Bixby's wandering scientist David seeks and then actually finds a man who also would turn into a Hulk, but an older generation previously earlier before. He finds him after hitchhiking through the part of America that has woods. The man went by the name of Dell Frye, and he was creepy. But he also had in his possession a cure against turning into the Hulk, which was what our David was after. Let me tell you something and you listen to me: when Dell Frye turned into the elderly Hulk, he was one of the scariest things I or you had ever seen. Not one of any of the perhaps tens of thousands of people who have ever lived have ever seen anything so frightening. Not even after going to Hell for a while. It's not hyperbole to say that. It's not. No. No. But the most fearsome part of the episode wasn't the old man transforming into an old Hulk, or the pitched battle between the young Hulk and the old in the nice Appalachian laboratory. It was David's tears when the elderly Hulk threw the vial containing the cure against the wall; the sound of David crying. I'd never really paid attention to people around me all my life until that episode, so I never saw the sight or heard the sound of a grown man crying before. No one had. When I think back on that Friday night on the CBS television network in March of 1981, what I realize is that I was afraid to watch all of the episode. What drove my fear? Why was I so scared? What was there to be afraid of? Me? I feared for everything: my life, my family and my father because The Incredible Hulk wasn't some show on some network. It was *reality*. What was happening was *real*.

Before There Were Mirrors

Tripping in saggy pants
beneath Neanderthal parasols
purchased in Louisiana,
this is what we used to look like.

Suspicious of every possible shadow
and constantly discovering Thanksgiving foods
such as turnip, maize juice and hazelnuts,
garter belts at the ready,
we used to wear tricorne hats,
standing on corners of earth that one day
would grow close to wild with streetlights like lichen.
We used to wear witchhunter hats with buckles on them,
kicking in the doors to lightning-struck chapels
in dark, numberless summers.

We somehow did not repulse each other;
we somehow made some more of ourselves
in Dickinson beds stained with Puritan oils,
itchy with lumber bark.

Squished in whalebone galoshes,
when we were colonial industrial children
we used to have to wear our washboards
and dunce caps all through church,
strawberry pie, strawberry pie,
trying to keep our monocles clean in the shower;
we used to wear long night shirts (um, gross much?)
breeches and kerchiefs,
we looked like awkward human dolls,
and yet we somehow found a way
to disregard what we wore
and propagated the species anyway.

We used to wear suspenders and linseed oil;
we used to wear hard tack and miter helmets;
it was any wonder at all that children came out of us.

Fish-market crazed and bustling about in miniature,
seriously we used to wear petticoats and hoops,
frocks the colour of white ghosts,
we men and women, of both kinds,
trapped in the decades we lived in,
we used to have to wear shifts and stays,

nervous and indigneous grass skirts,
and then the American Revolutionary Civil War happened
all during the eighteen-ninety-fours,
and so, as a consequence,
we used to wear chemises and muskets,
we used to wear bee bonnets
and ostentatious gramophone horns,
zoot suits and calliopes.
How could we have known,
slinky and pinched as we were,
what dreams of terrible were to come;
we used to wear bodices
made from pantaloons and ascots,
crying ourselves to lice-ridden sleep.

But then, in the Amish megastores
of the Roaring Twenties, we found neckerchiefs
and cummerbunds that reminded us
that we came from gentlemen's canes and clubs;
we used to wear bow ties made from natural corn
and bead chokers hand-stitched out of ancestral finger knuckles;
we used to wear bell-bottoms and harem dresses all at once,
Gibson girl headsets with the World War II mood rings,
we used to wear cotton gins in the deafening Winter;
that time we all looked like Teddy Roosevelt;
even the us of we who were women.

Angels, we are sorry, but we cannot bear the blame
for what you had to look at over the centuries;
you cannot shame us with what we could not know
and therefore had no power to alter; after all,
we had yet to be inventing the idea of the mirror.

Wholesome Television Memories

I always hated that one episode of Little House on the Prairie where, after rescuing a seriously ill, unconscious Reverend Johnny Johnson from his runaway wagon in a blizzard, an innocent, down-on-his luck high school bully I once had named Caleb puts on the clergyman's collar and devises a plan to fleece the charitable townsfolk of Walnut Grove; I always hated that one episode where Florence was hired as the church's maid against the wishes of Laverne DeFazio, that one episode where Dan Mateo, the Alphans' botanist, started turning into a murderous, disfigured ghost while the Riddler got taken over by an alien manifestation, that one episode where Helen Keller taught Nellie Oleson how to do sign language in the cornflower field and I discovered masturbation, that one episode where they found azure and cerulean bones in the bell tower and it caused my mother to want to be buried in Hazelnut Grove, that one episode where Melissa Sue Anderson had a flat tire in a bad neighborhood and got harassed by a committee of Amish youths until Jan became allergic to Tiger and I had to run for student body president against the both of them, that one episode where Mr. Hooper asked Big Bird to help Charles Ingalls open up the store for him, that one episode where celebrated shaman Namutebi Okoro moved from Uganda to Philbert Grove and was forced to marry Laura Ingalls while I watched, while they all tried to drown me and my dinosaur in Plum Creek, that one episode with the suicide of my friend from school, that one episode with my parents' funerals, that one episode where my marriage disappeared, that one episode where I started having a hard time believing in God.

Makeup Tips for the Eye of Horus

I thought they were actually demons
so I let the Neanderthal out of me and howled for blood;
I started hollering and yelling old man phrases after them
get the hell off my lawn and all that
even though I live with my girlfriend in her ex-husband's house,
and what little lawn we have is barely enough for anyone to get off of;
I didn't know if they were Jehovah's Witnesses or Jehovah's Door-to-Door
salesmen
but I stood my ground Florida-style with extra pulp and bellowed,
bellowed even though I hadn't shaved or Axed my body
and today's modern alchemists symbolize resistance to change
at an elemental level
with a line drawing, laid on its side, of Lady Gaga
hate-fucking Emily Post into oblivion;
like a man dispossessed I chased those three or four youths
away from my front door
and yes, I'll still use the term youths even though I'm almost forty-five
and the WWII vet at Wal-Mart would consider me a youth;
it turns out they were the new religious tract salesmen
but they were not selling seventh day advent anything at all;
they were selling that I should like what MTV has become now;
they were selling that I should be ready for the Syrian slap-chop apocalypse;
they were selling that I should start not knowing
the meaning of gender anymore
and in modern alchemy the symbol for fear of being wrong about a new
person's gender
is a line drawing, laid on its side, of a stick figure man in a skirt
in a wheelchair digging a grave;
they were selling that I should learn to speak like the modern young people
and begin to become ambiguous, that I should begin to be afraid of being exact,
that I should start thinking of asking for a clear, concrete yes or no
as being rude;
it was the best three in the afternoon ever and I had the day off;
I was just eating my cereal just in a t-shirt and just my boxers
and it was a dark and stormy night even though it was three in the afternoon;
I chased them out of my cul-de-sac on that overcast Thursday
like I was St. Anthony and they were a pack of demons
and I was running them away from here, forcing them off of Egypt's cliff;
I ran after them past the open living room windows of my neighborhood;
I heard the soap opera women crying in the daylight air,
wailing like the witches in the olden-time movies,
weeping with all due loudness and inconsolable
because it seemed like there was no one who could remember 1985;
I heard the octogenarian infomercials asking who was that masked man

as fiery spit flecks flew out of my muzzle as I chased them chased them
chased them
until they were at last and forever out of my empty
middle-of-the-workday driveway
and in today's secret, modern alchemy, *the symbol for ironic dissolution,*
the symbol for precipitative collapse into your own first, base element
is a drawing, laid on its side, of Lindsay Lohan wetting herself
while trying to light a joint in a world-famous elevator.

Histories of Vilena

Nestled within Vilena's verdant Anhinga Valley
lies buried the insistent, hand-blown town of DeMaya,
where my fathers raised me with my mothers,
all of whom farmed and harvested and fished their crops
for many peaceful centuries, centuries which continue
to happen to us, even into today.

In Vilena, they say that the Sun takes its time
rising to shine over the wine fields,
and each glass of celebration knows to give us back
some of that sunshine when a toast is made.

In Vilena, they say that women named Maria
are historical, and that they pound flowers against stone
until a Western filmmaker realizes that they are important,
and then a movie happens that will dominate the Academy Awards.

In Vilena, grandfathers read the messages from the dead
in the Christmas bonfires of ancient antiquity
and grandsons first learn appropriate fear of Columbus;
these grandfathers are the men who gave us our fathers.

I was born in the tiny country of Vilena,
and I have been born there ever since.

What Every Child Should Know

Fathers should talk to their sons,
and their daughters also,
about the birds and the bees.

The "birds and the bees talk"
should take place very early on,
so there are no surprises waiting,
and also so that the young people
can make conscious decisions about
whether or not to have information.

When a man and a woman
love each other very much,
sometimes birds will choose to land
on the bedroom windowsill
and watch what the man and the woman
do to each other physically,
because birds have no sense of decency.

When a man and a woman
love each other very much,
and after they have become married
inside of a pulpit church,
sometimes they will be killed to death
by an immoral, uneducated swarm
of atheist bumblebees that came here
all the way from the Africa.
While scrambling for both cover
and for their scattered clothes,
the man and the young woman
will be naked and unashamed, and screaming.
This is God's great vision for all of us.

What young people need to know
is that the physical intimacy
that two people in love
may wish to share with each other
can lead to attacks by entire schools
of rage-infested, beady-eyed grackles
that will henpeck their faces
into blood-spatter patterns around their noses
as they try to flee and run away
from the night-time senior prom gazebo.

The two young people
must really love each other,
and be ready to make a serious commitment.

When a man and a young woman
who love each other very, very much,
and who have been married in the sight of God
attempt to involve wild birds into their lovemaking,
it can cause accidents with their body parts
that are ordained by Heaven
and even sometimes this lovemaking
can result in one, or even *both* of the couple
losing the use of one, or even *both* of their eyeballs.
Then, shrieking and eye-less,
the couple, devoutly, must say prayers;
they must be ready and wanting
to welcome the child of a blessing
into their newly-handicapped union.

These are the facts of life
we so often hear about,
that we often never hear about.

Fathers, when they sit us down
as children by the fireside
with our pipes and glasses of brandy,
should be honest with us
about what bees are capable of doing
to innocent people;
fathers should be honest with us
about how terrible,
how bald and vicious
newborn robins can be.

After Meadow Moved Away

"Fill my eyes
O Lithium sunset
And take this lonesome burden
Of worry from my mind" - Sting

If you ask me, I'd say
the edge of the woods began
where I guess they were always *meant to*,
back behind that quiet Cape Code house
at the bottom of West Barkus Road,
the silent one the color of a long-forgotten avocado
at fifteen minutes to blood orange dusk,
those woods we thought of as *the real world*
when the calendar came to June,
the world we excitedly preferred
to the primary color jungle of the elementary school,
those Summer noons so vast and free
with the busy working world
driving in cars on the roads
far away from our time for make-believe,
and we all would converge behind that house
before looking for trouble in the trees together,
that place that used to be Meadow Shaw's home
that house that had to remain Meadow's home
for years in our minds even after she moved away.
We'd meet there after our mothers gave us our lunches
and march across that back yard and over the tree line together,
looking for whatever trouble the sunlight could land on
and we all liked her; she was one of us
one of our little gang
in our small army
and it never mattered that she was a girl
although there was magic in her being a girl
that we used to wonder about
walking home together
after her mother would call her in,
and we heard someone say at school
one frozen morning that Autumn
that her parents had to move
because of her father's job
and we were too young to do anything
but hate the pain we felt at losing a friend,
too young because jobs didn't just do things to grownups

jobs did things to the kids that belonged to the grownups

and in the summer that came after her,
we would still meet behind that house
as soon as we saw the sunlight going pale and fading,
and we would still walk into the dark together
(because what does friendship mean
if not that these are the people
you need with you when things get dark)
but it was never the same

and before Meadow moved away
the sound of near and distant birds and bees and airplanes
and the smell of jasmine and gasoline
dazzled me in the blinding blue of the middle of the day
in the silencing glare of the Summer sun
while I just stood there, lost in daydream
while Meadow spoke to me so softly
while a memory took root in me
but I didn't care much for June
or much for July or much for anything
after Meadow moved away.

Transference

The driver of the white ice cream truck
stops in the middle of the quiet street
and throws it into park, and waits.
From the far, other end of the silent street
here comes an ambulance, finally;
its driver stops alongside the ice cream truck.

The two drivers share a meaningful glance
through their vehicles' driver's side windows,
and then they get out to trade places.

Now the ambulance rolls, moves at a crawl
through late afternoon neighborhood dusks,
The Entertainer blaring across endless front lawns;
now the ice cream truck bullets its way
through every intersection with its lights alive,
its siren screaming at the squawking pedestrians.

Is the world we see with our eyes the only one?
The world we see with our eyes is not the only one.

The Private Dances of Tegillclut, New Hampshire

Everyone in Tegillclut went to school together
and all at once as children and as high school children.
Ringed by sturdy, recalcitrant pines, this town
remains balanced between Autumn and Winter,
plus there is a hardware store and pavilion in the middle.
When a freckled baseball cap child catches a cold here,
the entire town reaches for a handkerchief all at once
in slow, black-and-white synchronized motion.
You have to be very careful if you are living here.
This small town has that disease where fire grows naturally.
You must exercise caution and you must never
be the reason for a shameful secret to exist,
because secrets live almost as long as mosquitoes here.
A lot of nights here have almost dozens of stars in them.
Some nights here have only that one star by the half-moon.
Walk in the front door of Aphrodite's, on the edge of town,
under a night with no Moon to take you to your favorite seat.
How many singles, like ladder rungs slipping, do you have?
You fold your bills vertically and prop them up near your beer.
Vanessa is coming your way now, and her bikini is so pink
you can't even see her top under the thrumming neon.
It costs so, *so much* to be danced upon in this town.

Eight Deep Breaths

Ten minutes to eight on a Tuesday night,
I lie in bed trying to nap, or rise from a nap,
whatever the case may be, and my eyes can see
bright, shapeless blue stars dancing on the wall;
I look to the window, realize those are police lights
shining through my bedroom window;
someone's been pulled over by the cops in front of my home;
the sun is almost completely down, but it waits
until the police have gone before falling under the West.

•

On the car radio as I head to the store
I hear the song *96 tears* as I'm driving
and a memory of a hot summer afternoon
running and then leaping over a sprinkler
comes out of nowhere; suddenly I'm in tears,
missing people I've made no effort to keep in contact with
over the years; sometimes that broken heart you lug around
gets broken by your own foolish hands;
a light, early evening spring drizzle
throws a rainbow on the road in front of me;
the bottles of wine clink in the bag
on the passenger-side floor of the car.

•

I say thank you miss to the girl who picks up the bag I drop
as I'm leaving the supermarket
and she shoots me a pretty, young glare
and then spits on me: *don't call me miss* she says
and suddenly I feel too heavy to keep standing up;
the world spins and my knees buckle; it's not an earthquake
but something in my heart wants to just give up;
I only called her what I was raised to call her,
but she and her generation dislike even polite titles
if they happen to come from the lips of old men they do not know;
I raise my eyes to the sky just in time to catch it happening up there;
I watch as rust forms on the pearly gates in rapid, fast-forward motion
and all the lights go out in Heaven.

•

The little town I grew up in,
on the furthest right edge of America,
was not too far from a natural wonder called Purgatory Chasm,
a series of huge and rocky gashes opening up the world,
a hospital's worth of wounds right in the middle of a national forest;
a sprawling gallery of craggy stone vulvas split wide among ferns
that you could climb down into
and feel the hot breath of the earth on your neck;
I remember there was a rock formation called The Devil's Pulpit
in the center of that dreamscape in green and gold and grey,
a cylindrical promontory thrusting up from the ground
only four feet high; I used to clamber over to it
and play like I was about to preach to some invisible flock
but no real words would ever come; I would only ever start laughing
and hear my mirth echo in the trees; there was just no way
that summer could ever come to an end.

•

I cannot wait to die.
I'm excited for the prospect of rasping
that last breath out of my colorless body
and I dream of a dozen ways that I won't live anymore:
the whole world on its bloody, strewn-glass side
as I lie under an overturned truck on some highway,
the bathroom lights suddenly leaping skyward
as the shower drain hurls itself up to my face
and then just blackness, just the sound and feel of blackness,
not even that blackness, actually, just
the deepest sleep one could ever hope for.

•

When it was just the neighbor's kids and me and my sisters
on that rickety, screened-in porch of my mother's neighbor's house,
when we were little, snickering and thoughtless,
we would play at conducting séances, foolish,
in heavy summer thunderstorm afternoons
and why on earth wouldn't we have done so,
since the afternoon sky was already that dark, sick green it would get
when the late July lightning and rain tore it apart?
We'd ask former president John F. Kennedy,
and anyone else we could think of who died
to kindly make some sound, rap their afterlife knuckles

on the underside of the table, make our glasses of Kool-Aid
shake and tremble with the force of their deceased annoyance;
there was no better love you could have back then for your brother
than to show him how far you were willing to go to frighten him.

•

There's a spider clinging to the ceiling just above the fan,
trying to hold her own against the whirlwind we've created
with our need to make a breeze in the house; it's not even June yet;
we've got a month to go before the summer comes;
we have years to go before we will feel our last summer in this house;
we have whole lives to live before we come to some agreement
about who is allowed to die first between us;
we have all the time in the world
to learn how to love each other again,
over and over again.

Let Us Remember Whoever This Was

He was my blond uncle,
and he was a good, blond man.
He was stronger than any animal
you ever saw lift weights.
He walked proudly around our town
with tissuey, patriotic bunting
trailing loosely from his waist
because that's just the kind of man
he always just happened to be.
He built the Statue of Liberty every day
with his bare, pink hands and then
he allowed the French to give it to us;
here was a man who was at least just as American
as any immigrant who was American ever was,
right up until the time he wasn't no more.
He, my uncle, was a man who stood for
whatever he stood for even if he didn't always know
what it was that he proudly stood for,
and we were all very proud of him
for the strength to believe in his own convictions.
I would tell you what his name was,
but he was loved by so many of us
that it really doesn't even matter
what his name was, or what we called him.
Some people called him a plumber,
but those of us who knew him
knew him as a son, a father, an uncle,
a husband, and in some cases, an aunty.
Those of us who really knew him
often thought of him as a surgeon,
and, once in a while, as a good friend.
And this man lived a good, classic American life
right up until that dark, chocolate Saturday
when he was taken from our clutches too soon
by a disease that doesn't play favorites
but knows all too well who it likes to kill the most.
He was gone from us at the tender forty-year-old age.
The doctors say it was the late onset
of sudden infant crib syndrome
but I can't bring myself to believe them,
even though I know they are doctors.

Here was a man who was both
an uncle, and, apparently,
a man I knew somehow.
Remember him.

Cutting Myself, Shaving

I've only been awake for ten minutes
and I already have a razor in my hand.
The pale cadmium of the lights
lit above the bathroom sink
make my face flesh fearful
in that tired image in the glass
as I watch myself touch
the spot on my chin where I've drawn blood,
as I watch the cloud cover of shaving cream
turn an unnerving coral hue;
it's almost six in the morning
and I can see my father in the mirror
standing right behind me;
now I look small again
and he is showing me how to do it,
how to hold the blade to my skin,
showing me how to cut away
what has been given leave
to grow for too long.
His voice is calm, as though
this moment has come
right when he expected it to,
but I hear the lost animal of fear
in his voice, as well, as though
he knows I'll draw blood on the first try.
He is right; I nick myself on the chin,
and we watch the little red raindrop
spatter and ping into the palm of the white basin,
we both share a nervous laugh, a moment
and then he is gone, it's half past six
and I am right on time
for almost being late to work.
I let the water run cold
to rinse away that drop of my blood,
which is just as much my father's blood
as it is my own, and so I wake myself,
snap myself out of whatever this is
with that same cold water.

Watch for Slow, Icy Children

Right and left shoulder roads closed; do not enter.
Roads closed only one way; do not enter or yield.
Roads closed due to crossing pedestrians yielding to flaggers;
stop and slow down the divided highway ahead.
Thirty-five miles per hour child pedestrian crossing;
do not enter, yield to or drive through child.
You may not make a left turn.
You may not make an icy or divided left turn.
You may not turn right, either.
You may not be a large truck.
You *must* be a large truck; you just *have* to be.
You must be a slow, childlike pedestrian truck
who will not yield or enter or watch for falling rock.
But this isn't just about what you can or can't do, or be;
slow children, too, may not drive trucks to the left;
that pedestrian road is closed to slow children.
Watch those slow children close the road for a leaping deer.
Be prepared to stop those slow children.
Be prepared to stop the slow, icy children with a weight limit of eight tons.
Be prepared to bump slow children who will not yield to leaping deer,
or to boulders falling, or to crossing pedestrians.
Be prepared for photo-enforced tractors crossing a winding, icy dead end.
Be prepared to photo-enforce the crossing of winding, icy children.
Be prepared to stop and slow down as you cross through
the playground full of deer and flaggers and utility men,
for there is no hitchhiking allowed along the hiking trail
unless the boulders that are falling allow cattle to cross.
Be prepared for four-way dead ends that are sharp, slippery and oncoming.
Be prepared to yield to oncoming national forests,
and hairpin railroads with low clearance and high visibility.
Be prepared for the fact that dangerous, icy children
might come out of a national forest and weigh you.
Do not yield or fail to yield or yield to the failure
of that slippery, national, oncoming road.

A Scary Time

In the middle of the day on a Friday afternoon in the first week of August in the Summer of 1981, when I was only thirteen years old, my mother accidentally put me in the washing machine with some dirty clothes and put me through two full wash cycles. At four foot eleven I was a little short for my age, and I guess I was easy to miss among the beach towels and jeans. I forgive her now and I forgave her that day. There was a lot going on. My mom was between jobs. Believe it or not, the theme from The Greatest American Hero was the number one hit song in the United States. I was home from school. Dad was at work. It was a scary time. America was a little girl crouching in fear of the bomb behind a box of Mary Lou Retton Wheaties and crack cocaine had yet to be born. I remember flailing my arms and screaming but I don't think mom heard me. I looked up from the hot water just as the lid was closing down, and I held my breath in the dark soap. For the next dizzying and brutal forty-five minutes, I was washed mercilessly. The holes in the metal of the tub flayed my skin at first and I had to hug the plastic fin tight until the cycle was over. Seemed like it took forever for the water to drain and be gone. I tried to cry out for help but all that came out of my mouth were soap bubbles, each one containing only a fragment of the scream I was trying to make. When each bubble contacted the rim of the machine, it would burst and let out only a snippet of my scream. Then there was light and I saw my mother reach for a towel to inspect it for cleanliness. She frowned in concentration and didn't even seem to see me there. I remember seeing from my vantage point the top of the green, red and cream box of biodegradable *Safe brand detergent*. She reached for it and dusted me right in the eyes as she added more soap. Then I saw the lid close again. I tried to kick the machine to get her attention but I was stuck in a fetal position and could do no harm. She wanted us to have clean clothes and I had to respect that. After the second cycle, another agonizing forty-five minutes in the water, she pulled all the clothes out and found me. She patted my back until I sputtered and thanked her for saving me. *Whoops*, she said, *I'm so sorry about that. It's okay, Mom*, I said, and we hugged. I was fine. It was just a little bit upsetting.

Whisperville

I am driving a very brown,
economy luxury sedan, unmarked,
all the perilous way down
the winding, afternoon-lit road
around the perimeter of Whisperville,
a well-known gated community here by the city,
and I glance out the window
at the high, grey stone wall
which completely, irrevocably
circles the homes in there.
It takes me fifteen minutes to an hour
to drive all the way around the place,
and as I do, I think about the things
people have told me about this private area;
the barbershop says you can't go in there
unless you know somebody;
the police department says you can't go in there
unless you make a lot of money;
the church says some of the mothers in there
look pretty good in their white tennis skirts and visors;
my mailman says telekinetic children
swing on swings near little school pools of water,
and that ducks walk past them in a single-file line,
blindly following encrypted, secret orders
that emanate from camouflaged antennas.
I make the final turn
to complete the loop around.
As if on cue, a handful of angry bees
are suddenly in my car; I'm waving my hands
trying to shoo them away from my face;
because of these bees, I lose control of the car
and I nearly plow right into one of the walls;
instead, I choose to correct my course
and get back on the road; predictably,
the bees fly out the passenger window;
the crisis is over for now.
It's Fall, the leaves are a wet collage
on either side of the road
and I have to brake hard sometimes.
Fighting back tears, I'm laughing
as I hear an old Rodney and Dangerfield song
on the radio that's in my car;
it doesn't matter how many times they tell me
what the people do to each other in there;

it doesn't matter how often I've heard
how they talk to one another in there;
something in that place has attracted me
like pheromones in the park, and I drive
until the needle approaches "E", every day,
trying with all of my might to live there.

All of This Candy Belongs to Me

All of this candy belongs to me, child.

Look at all these hard, hot cinnamon pinwheels
and the sticks of chewy caramel in my hand;
you may have none of it, not even one piece,
not the lemon gum nor the raspberry nougats either
and making your eyes get wider won't change my mind.

This banana-flavored lollipop tastes amazing,
a joy your tongue will never know, little child.
You can whimper; piteously plead all you like
and I'll meet your eyes with mine while I lick this licorice whip.
Has it begun to rain, or are those tears on your cheeks?
There's plenty of this blue cotton candy to go around,
but I'm not going to let it go around to you, child.

Stamping your feet and crying won't work with me;
I will bite the head off this chocolate bunny and then
I'll tell you all about how good and chocolatey his life was
while you lick your jealous lips in the rain.

Why am I being like this?

Because you still have the sweetness of your childhood to savor,
while I must suck on this cherry cane and try to remember mine.

II.
Green Apple Jolly Ranchers

Nighthawk Blues

There's an all-night diner on the corner of Green and Washington forever, a few blocks down, always, from the Diamond Tavern and I'm almost there. I couldn't sleep; I still can't sleep; I might never sleep again. I walk, exhausted, from my apartment in the Lexington district all the way down here. I get a few blocks from the place and I stop at the park near Preston Gardens and I look up. The sky is still there, but it looks like it just got there a few minutes ago. Some of the stars in the sky are just waking up, and some of the stars in the sky are just getting ready to go to sleep. I know I'm not a star in the sky; I keep moving, and the closer I get to the diner the more the streetlights go out, the less light there is and then after a couple blocks' worth of total darkness I see the warm glow from the diner pouring out onto the corner; I look in the windows and see a redheaded woman in a red dress having a cup of coffee at the red counter. She's beautiful but she isn't alone; she's with a man and they're deep inside their own conversation. I get it: this part of town is composed of my insomnia and wanderlust and I push myself through the door. It's ninety-nine cents for a Coke or a coffee here; it's ninety-nine cents for a dream on rye; it's ninety-nine cents to go back in time. I make the redhead's gentleman companion disappear with a wish and take a seat beside her. There's no sound coming from the empty benches on the midnight street outside the windows and I fall, holding on to every year I've ever lived, into the gleaming crimson of her lips; I might never sleep again.

After I Eat An Edible from Colorado, Neil deGrasse Tyson Somehow Narrates My Late Night Munchies Trip to the Kitchen

It may be a startling thing to reflect upon, but maybe we humans should be comforted by the knowledge of our place in all of existence. After all, our galaxy, the Milky Way, is really just a speck in our universe and that universe is but *one* universe among thousands of other universes, and each of these universes contain galaxies so large, so full of constantly-moving and vibrating atoms, that if you were to try to think about it even for one minute, your brains would turn into burnt cookie dough or mashed potatoes.

But what if all those atoms in space, still cooling even now from the Big Bang and still without a name, what if all those small, hot molecules of wonder somehow bursting into carbon life forms over the millions of eons wound up *here*, in this kitchen, at just the right time for you to join them in search of nachos? Come with me aboard the *Ship of The Imagination,* where no laws of dynamic science can prevent us from finding out just what there is to eat in here…

Right now, on the Cosmic Calendar, it's *12:45 am*, forty-five minutes after midnight, and you are hungrier than you have ever been in your lifetime, as the edible you ate expands your horizon and turns your jaw into a whirling merry-go-round of synthesizers and taste buds. And it is in this very moment that the very notion of nachos first occurs to you. And like all good ideas, this one comes just as you are hurtling through the *space-tile continuum* of your kitchen at an astonishing zero kilometers a second, or, to put it another way, 23 millimeters a second. It would take you 15 light years to begin moving faster than you are now. As the earth slowly cools and begins to form a delicious graham cracker crust, you begin to laugh at the face in the microwave as you coast along the counter at twice the speed of margarine, or, to put it another way, over two-hundred times one-fourth the speed of Doritos.

Let's diverge off this path for a moment to ask ourselves one question: How did the Doritos even *get here?* Did they arrive, as some believe, because a system of stars made of nacho and cheese finally grew too heavy and collapsed in on itself in a furious and cosmically tasty *condiment horizon,* or could the answer to this question be that you drove to Albertsons a few hours ago and bought some Doritos and you forgot? As you stand here wondering this, a whole new jar of sliced jalapenos is evolving in your refrigerator. Did this just happen by chance? Or did the refrigerator begin to evolve to survive in your kitchen over the billions of years, once it learned that its very survival depended on containing snacks that you liked to eat? Logic tells us that the laws of nature and gravity must have allowed for the sliced jalapenos to exist, to be thrown onto a plate of Doritos and cheese, and, one day, maybe even this very night, to wind up *inside of you.*

And as your curious mind theorizes on all these scientific inquiries in your kitchen, just wearing your pants and no shirt, you stand on the shoulders of those who theorized before you: Einstein, Faraday, Newton, Copernicus and Galileo in what could perhaps be thought of as *the ugliest cheerleader pyramid ever seen by human eyes*.

We are now cruising through the *taste-time continuum* at the speed of a few glasses of Guinness, five Slim Jims and two handfuls of cashews. *Is that some leftover popcorn over there?*

Come with me, aboard the *Ship of The Imagination*.

Dizzy Was Dizzy
(tribute to Gillespie written while a speculative science show
 about physics and whatnot was playing in the other room)

Dizzy Gillespie was an accomplished jazz trumpet player
who was the greatest jazz trumpet player alive
during the years around 1940 when he was arguably alive.
Even so, people are clueless about what made the Big Bang happen.
People think that energy just comes from out of thin where.
People think that time travel is very impossible, but it's not;
it's actually very close now to being almost not impossible.
People can't and don't understand that the reason
that Dizzy was called Dizzy was because
Dizzy was born with two twin ear canals,
one for each ear, and thus due to his lack of balance
he thus lived his entire life thus afraid of stairwells
and other things in life that could make him thus
lose his balance from the height of however tall he thus was.
Whoa, Dizzy. Careful, there, okay?
People think it's a joke that Dizzy was dizzy,
but people like that should be executed
until they are electric-chaired to death
because they don't understand that
sometimes people are born able to be dizzy
at all of the hours of the day and of the night,
except that they might don't not want to be dizzy like that;
Dizzy was arguably the greatest player of the jazz trumpet
who was able to accidentally fall down just from standing up for a minute.
Sometimes black holes would lose their theoretical balance
and fall into Dizzy when Dizzy was on top of a jazz stage,
bebopping on his musical trumpet like as though it was
a kind of melodical instrument of mass inflection;
Dizzy played sometimes music that made up be down;
this is how we get our modern concepts of mass, energy, and mass.
When Dizzy Gillespie was famous in the world,
the whole world wrote entire letters to the Vatican Pope
to pray for him and to ask the Pope to force Jesus to help Dizzy
be not so damned dizzy all the time, because Dizzy
would sometimes fall down these long, miraculous flights of stairs
on the way to the stages that he would be asked to play on;
sometimes Dizzy was so dizzy that he would fall *up* flights of stairs,
he would fall *up* flights of stars also too; he would fall up into the air
off of these stages he would be on, playing his jazz metal trumpet
even as he was floating up over all the jazz people,
and sometimes then Dizzy would get so dizzy
that all the people below him would lose their balance, too,

and this is how modern television and bebop jazz became born.
What is our role in the universe, and when did time begin?
People should oughta be arrested and injected into jail
for asking stupid questions like that instead of living and working.
Right now Dizzy Gillespie is a guy in heaven,
and he's still dizzy, even up there in his afterdeath,
wailing on his jazz harp like as if it were a heavenly trumpet
like all the bible people talk about in the Bible,
and all the angel people up there in the heavens,
billowy and, um, thin in their Downy-soft angel sheets,
all of them are getting dizzy from being near Dizzy,
all of them from being able to hear Dizzy
and even now some of these dizzy, Downy angels
are losing their white, cottony-soft balances
and tumbling over the edges of clouds,
falling down to natural, atmospheric Earth,
which is a planet that turns around a lot;
Dizzy used to live there.

Something like Eight Hundred

They want to be artists, these people.

They come around my house, all the time,
snapping pictures of me in artistic (I guess) *almost-focus*
as I haul my garbage bags like corpses down my driveway,
and those pictures get hung up on the walls
of that museum in the city downtown,
which I guess for someone is great,
but those stolen glimpses of me can't be art.
I'm only one guy, one regular-sized regular guy;
I got no idea what these people are doing.

They steal my fingerprints
right off the handle on the door of my car
and negative-print them onto transparencies,
and then they project them onto a wall
at some club somewhere while some band is playing;
these people are sleeping in a tent
right outside of my bedroom window
pretty much every night of the god-damned week,
and they make field recordings of my snoring,
and then they make songs out of those recordings
and release them with all my breaths for percussion
to all the local college radio stations
and I have to hear my own stupid snoring
when I'm changing the station in my car
but I never told them they could do that!

I ask them, repeatedly, not to do these things
but they tell me that I "inspire" them,
that I have no idea how "interesting" I am,
that even the little things I do everyday
are worthy of a drawing, or a sketch, or a song.

I don't want to inspire *anybody*.

What do *I* wish for?

I wish those kids would stop coming around
to cover me up with papier-mâché;
I don't even know why they picked me.
Just last week I found out
that they shot something like eight hundred,
maybe a thousand hours of footage,

just of me washing my dishes,
just of me walking down the hallway
in my deep, mummified sleep
listing side to half-awake side
in the direction of the teakettle's monastic drone,
scratching my balls through my pajamas
in the late weekend mornings;
it's not a good feeling to be told
by a friend on the phone
that *there's a new statue of your head*
at an art gallery somewhere;
it's an even stranger not good feeling
to go to that gallery and check out
that painted clay version of your own head up close
on top of a wooden pedestal with a little white card under it,
to look into those dotless, doppelgänger eyes,
to hear strangers whisper to each other
how much they like your forehead,
how they really love the look in your eyes,
how intensely you seem to stare.

Fight

The next day, I was walking along the city's pretty avenue
when I spied, right there, carefully, in the middle of the road,
two men going *toe-to-toe*: they were fighting to the real death.
It was very bloody and my eyes bled, also, to see such violence.

The taller of the two men was surely in his early young twenties.
He was pale and strapping, and wore a muscle tee and NY cap.
He was of the race *dudebro,* and his forearms and biceps shone
with sweat in the Sun as he punched and parried in the brawl.

The shorter of the two men was easily about 5 or 6 years old.
He was just under four feet tall, and his red hair and freckled cheeks
shimmered in the light as he ducked and lunged and growled, spit
flying from his lips as he took and gave vicious punches and kicks.

The taller man landed a boot in the shorter man's chest, sending
him sprawling backwards into a post office drop box at the corner.
The shorter man screamed, clutched his chest, then rallied, rolling
to the side and firing a balled fist up into the groin of the taller one.

The twenty-three-year-old wheezed and his eyes bulged so hard
it seemed like they were about to snap right off the stalks. Still,
he managed to catch and hold the six-year-old's head in his hands
in the tight scuffle, and he pressed his thumbs down into the eyes.

The six-year-old, in return, cried and grabbed the older one's nipple
and twisted it clean off, getting blood all over the both of them.
Their battle kicked up a lot of dust and trash in the street, and soon
they were surrounded by a swirling brown cloud and invisible to me.

As I watched this go on, I noticed that my Coca-Cola tasted funny.
It tasted like the girl working at the soda fountain failed to make sure
there was enough syrup to make the soda right. I winced in irritation.
How annoying that I was going to have to run all the way back there.

Be on the Lookout

I've had the news on since 9. The television screen has been yapping, of course, nonstop screeching about the horrible news. One more murder, another killing by the serial killer on the prowl in this beautiful, modern, verdant and once-peaceful city I've called my home. This hip town. This chic burg. A paradise turned to landfill in a fortnight. In the basement, where my laundry is done, I heard at noon from the radio I keep going down there that the police have no new leads. A total of three things is what they only now know. The killer uses the same type and brand of hatchet for each job. They know this. They know he's a he. And the killer, they know, always catches the victims in the lemon-scented, blissful privacy of their own homes. While the latest, this last night's killing, is still hot, so fresh in the buzzing, dusty mind, the others keep one on the edge of the couch as well. In the last several weeks, the killer, visibly irritated, has butchered a left-handed mime known well in the international district for busking, a breastfeeding rights advocate woman with albinism, an overweight, alt-right conspiracy nut infamous for blogging the phone numbers of the members of city council, a redheaded college girl known and beloved throughout the community and under investigation for her volunteer efforts for the exploding homeless veteran population, two schoolchildren waiting in the morning rain on their porch for the bus to arrive, and a gay, wealthy real estate magnate who just happened to be in the kitchen of one of his many homes at the time of his execution. The pattern couldn't be clearer. There can be no doubt; the killer goes after a specific type. Everything fits. I'm next.

Mercury's Children

The motorcycles scream past my house,
right around one a.m. every night.
And what could anyone's hurry be so late?
So many evenings it's the same, as though
this were some game of chess
in which I am made to confess
that I will never know what the rush is.
What is this all about?
The way the dandelion falls apart
with a blown kiss in the wind;
it's almost always too fast for me.
There was once a time, in this world,
when people marveled at how quickly the mail came,
months after the ink dried,
when the mail came on the back of a horse.
See the slow motion film of a rose opening over time;
sing the first six notes of Ave Maria in your mind.
An ice cube, eventually a little lake
on a picnic table top in the middle of July.
One candle's flame, shivering, quivering
and surrounded by a silent, black night.
Look at me.
The tiny blonde college girl approaches,
and opens her mouth.
She speaks to me with a cell phone against her ear.
I take her by the hand and drag her into the trees.
I crush her phone under a stone and make her
listen to the world of the woods for an afternoon.
And after, I return her to her world,
with a commandment to spread the word:
God is not the father of these people around you:
slow down.
The man, the man in the white pickup truck
honks at the man ahead of him
for taking too long to see that the light has turned green.
Boldly, and with purpose, I step off of the sidewalk.
Before his foot is on the gas pedal, I open the door
and pull the pickup driver outside.
I pull down his pants. I give him a firm 3 spankings
and send him on his way with my new prayer book,
on every page of which is one single line of print:
God is not the father of these people around you,
slow down.
If the ideas these images represent confound or offend

is it only because they delay Mercury's children today.
The history books tell us that one day, long ago,
Superman turned the Earth the other way around,
for love, to stop love from dying.
Until the day the scientists find a way to do this,
until that revolution, all we can do
is try to stop love from dying, so,
slow down.

Right Under Our Noses

There is an alien living next door to my house.
Through both his windows and curtains I see him,
and even though he looks like a human sort of person
with his actual hair and eyes, his skin and living fingers,
I can still figure out by what he does what he is.

Call me paranoid, but I don't see it that way
when, in the sights of my telescope at night,
even at the latest, oddest hours on the clock,
when everyone else in the neighborhood is deep asleep,
I've caught him walking around half-dressed.

Sometimes, when I watch him through the hole
I drilled into the roof and ceiling over his bedroom,
he makes these prayers to angels with weird names
that I don't know and I've never seen him kneel;
I think it's clear this guy isn't from around here.

It's very disturbing to listen to the recordings
I've made of him with the bug I planted in his pillow
and discover that sometimes he talks on the phone
to people that I don't know about since I'm not him;
I'm afraid all day long that he's the evil kind of alien.

Once in a while I'll catch him brushing his teeth
in the camera I installed in his bathroom mirror,
and he doesn't brush his teeth the way I like to;
there's something very wrong, very different in him
and I worry about the things I'm going to have to do.

He eats breakfast foods I can't bring myself to recognize;
nights he pleasures himself alone to sights I find repugnant;
when I go through his mail I find pink envelopes
from the places where all the strangers come from,
and, honestly, I'm pretty much at my wit's end over here.

I've tried to talk with him about my concerns
but every time I do, I can only get as far as
thinking about talking with him about my concerns
before I remember that I put a webcam in his shower;
I'm running out of time; what am I supposed to do?

Miracle in the Food Court

Suppose you could levitate a woman into the air
somewhere clear and safe, someplace America enough
to be in the middle of a crowded Indiana food court
at some shopping mall in some trusted where,
somewhere in the middle of some insured and American America
nestled deep in some kind of Indiana somewhere in some food court;
suppose you could do it, suppose you could lift her up in the air
perhaps twenty feet or around so, just by using only your intentions only
and disrobe her then, slowly disrobing her
article of clothing by article of clothing,
using only the powers of your mind
as you appear to everyone outside of you
as simply that person studying that map of the mall
at the outer frontier of the food court:
first will go her independent, chunky black shoes,
and then her well-worn, pale blue jeans
that hugged her form so damned well
and then her white, not guilty ruffly socks,
and then her black sweater that's interfered too long,
and then her dark red bra of all her august, glistening sins,
and then her dark red panties that pulse like butterfly wings;
suppose you could do this evil
and be this devious, dismantling her modesty;
let's suppose you could do this
as all the eaters in the food court watch,
letting their drinking straws fall out of their lips,
as all the clocks stop what they are doing, in shock;
let's suppose you could hold her up
ten feet or fifteen maybe in the air
and expose her body until she is up there on an invisible cross,
surround by a hundred unwilling disciples,
a hundred Judases with Orange Julius drinks in their hands;
let's suppose you really could do all of this,
would you find yourself worrying that people will see them,
the invisible and obvious pearls in your eyes,
that they will see that you are the one with the blue guilt in your veins,
that you are the one with the bad, bad telekinesis,
that you are the one raising her?

Why do you worry so much
over things you cannot control?

Trying to Remember Your Name after Amazing Sex

I do all that I can to recall
every time I've been there
to witness the moment
when you met someone
for the first time; sometimes
it's hard to hear you over the din
of doorbells and other people
in my memories; I try to rewind
these memories and stop them
right at the moment you're about
to tell a stranger who you are,
but the mix tape inside of me
seems like it's been recorded over
in spots with the reports of faraway guns;
I wish we lived in a home so large and grand
that every time we ran into each other
in the hallway we'd be meeting for the first time again;
I'm pretty damned wealthy because of your love
but I still think it would be fun
to have so much money
I could throw pieces of real gold
into the garbage disposal and turn it on;
I wish I could fly like a steroid hero
and carry you over the city,
then drop you just to hear you scream,
then catch you just to hear you cry
and then make you only remember
the part where I saved your life;
look at me with those eyes of yours
and try to guess what I am thinking.
You and I could live in a town
without ambulances if we wanted to.

Whatever your name is, I'd go back in time
if you were with me, that much I know.
Wait. Don't say anything.
Don't say anything other than *please*.
I know who you are now.

You're the one I'm brave for
when it comes to big spiders on the wall,
daddy long legs behind the wine bottle on the counter;

I hope you thought my hesitation at saying your name
was simply me trying to catch my breath,
because you'd be right.

Whenever I Get An Idea,
A Light Bulb Full of Gunpowder
Appears Above My Head

through the window
at this moment
an unsettling sight:

all over this neighborhood
made from genuine and authentic
tan suburban afternoon,
houses are dismantling themselves
in slow motion

you can see it

debris rising up into the sky
everywhere you look

beds, dressers, walls, sconces,
sinks still full of water, roofs, chairs,
everything and all else that isn't everything
floating up into an overcast
the color of an unplugged light bulb

so when the salesman pounds on my door
and rings the bell at the same time,
what am I supposed to do?
supplicate? listen carefully to his pitch?
appreciate his enthusiasm?
why doesn't he notice
what I can see plain as day out there?
aren't there more pressing matters
needing our attention?

if, from here on out, it becomes necessary
to live in that inclement, vibrating and emotional hospital
where the people who can't think right anymore
wind up spending the rest of their lives,
I want it to be my decision.

Still Fruit, with Life

Wow, how the honey claws
of the little wicker basket
on my countertop all this last week
carried lots of fruit for me to take with,
in the silence of a house not quite awake,
on the long, lightless way to work,
with the scales of a dream
descending, still falling from my eyes;
there were two plums
and a little cloud of grapes in there.
Also, there was a small cabal of bananas,
which, by Friday morning,
became, simply, one final banana
with the shadows all grown into it;
how those spots appeared in the peel,
seemingly at the same rate of speed
as the getaway car to work
my dreams were last seen in.

Home Improvement

Dollar bills keep pouring out
of the kitchen faucet every time
I go to fill the sink for dishes
or to fill up the water bowl for the cat
and concerned a bit I sure am right now
because not only there should be water
coming out where the money is coming in
but the city, the city that leaflet-yells at us
about how much water we use in the summer
the city that has kind of a police force problem
the city where some of the hardest working people
are the everyday folks engaged in criminal enterprise,
I wonder if the city will find out somehow
that I have constant dollar bills on tap here;
it's been happening since about ten a.m.,
a lot of dollars, a lot, a stressing mayhem.
I wouldn't have noticed this
if I didn't have the day off and now
my lady and I have had, sadly,
to swear each other to lover's secrecy
and hope that this doesn't last
and hope that this lasts long enough
for us to get a couple of things
we have been wanting around the house.
The dollar bills flow so fast
from the faucet. You can't even believe it.
It's a pale, sage-green breeze
coming out of there; listen,
you have to promise me
you won't tell anyone;
I'll get you whatever you like
just please just
shhhhh.

Recalling the Weight

Bolted to the back top corner
of my garage is a grey steel pulley.
It squeaks a little from time to time.
Sometimes my mind imagines it smiling.
Bolted to the front top corner
of the shed behind the garage
is yet another pulley entirely.
It makes its own song when it hears
pulley number one clearing its throat.
Strung and run through these two pulleys
is a fraying length of grey, cotton clothesline.
There's a distance of several yards
of wide open sunlight between
the front of the shed and the back of the garage.
Open sky, midday sunlight
of the loudest, most Summerest kind.
Emotional sunlight in which t-shirts dance
like they have a Louisiana ghost twitch.
On the leisurely days when my hands arrive
to hang a load or two of my wet, washed shirts,
the pulleys squeak like baby infant birds
waking up at the end of some Winter.
This story about my clean clothes
swaying, drying on the line in the sun
has been reenacted and retold ad mausoleum
throughout the course of my years
in this house that has lived with me here,
this house that looks just like the picture of the house
in the book of pictures of what houses look like.
The clothesline has quietly, saintily endured
many late afternoons of night-scented, slanting rain
like the rain on the canister of Morton's salt.
If only my night times were that exact colour blue.
If only I was as smart as that girl with the umbrella.
Now there was a girl who knew to plan ahead.
Me? I never thought to buy some nylon cord
for pulleys that moan and squeal in shadow and light.
When I look close I see the tired cotton recalling the weight;
I can see the tears and rips in the fabric of my line,
the rips and tears in the fabric on my mind,
and all my laundry hangs in the balance.

Overnight Sensation

My girlfriend thinks every old white man
she sees who has a bit of gray in his hair
(or who has a lot of gray in his hair)
(or who just has salt-and-pepper hair)
and a trimmed white or gray mustache
and who looks to be in his '70's or '80's
is Stan Lee, the famous comic book writer.
While Stan Lee is widely known to wear
a pair of dark black, difficult-to-miss eyeglasses,
the men she points out to me all over town
don't even need to be wearing vision correction
for her to shoot me the look, for her to believe
we're having a celebrity sighting over here;
her only requirement is they be six feet tall
or nearly so and be white and have a mustache,
and even on these matters she's growing
increasingly open to discussion and flexible.
She does this to me all the time, this fun game,
when we're out in public - that quick,
surreptitious leaning in very close to my side first
and then the carefully-timed whisper:
hey, look - that's Stan Lee over there,
and when I turn around to see for myself
I'll inevitably find an older man
who, yes, happens to be white
and who, yes, happens to be sporting a mustache
but those will be the only criteria
the individual in question will satisfy;
I have seen so many different kinds of Stan Lees
because of her: overweight Stan Lees, redneck
Stan Lees, dwarf Stan Lees, biracial Stan Lees
in overalls, Stan Lees that have full beards:
I'm starting to think from here on out
I'll need to start bringing one of my old comics
with me for an autograph just in case
she turns out to be right on one of these occasions.
And then other times I realize I have nothing
at all to be worried about, because her concept
of what Stan Lee really actually looks like
continues to broaden and diversify:

hey, look - that's Stan Lee over there

I heard it again the other day,
and this time when I turned to take a gander
I couldn't find the comics icon anywhere,
and there was only one person in that aisle
in the supermarket at the time:

love, are you talking about that Asian-American
woman in the motorized shopping cart?

Every trip to the market for bread and milk
has become a spy caper with absolutely nothing at stake,
no danger to anything but our sides from the laughing.

She tells me to hold on and be cool,
so she can ask if a picture together
wouldn't be an imposition.

The Silent Killer

Stricken with vandalism at the age of ten,
little Brian was terribly hobbled and ill-behaved
because of the congenital condition he got born with;
he tried to walk everywhere on his own,
but his disease caused him to have to stop
and deface some property with the spray paint can
he was born holding in his right hand.
His mother could do nothing but let him do it,
and pay the owners of the property after.
When the delivery doctor saw little Brian exit his mother
with a spray paint can in his hand, he knew something was wrong.
A lot of times, property owners would get mad,
but then they would look at little Brian's little face
and see that he just couldn't help being born
with a spray paint can in his hand,
and so then they would sort of pathetically smile
and let little Brian fulfill his disease against their belongings.
The child doctors tried to force little Brian to wear
a pair of metal, anti-vandalism arm braces,
but little Brian's disease gave him incredible strength,
and he wound up hurting a lot of doctors.
All that anybody could do was let little Brian do what he had to
and destroy the things that did not belong to him;
he had a disease that was incurable and unstoppable.
Everybody had to let little Brian ruin things.
Little Brian was a little boy who had snack crumbs on his mouth
and who defaced property everywhere he went
and you wanted to smack him but you couldn't.
I'm sorry, but you could never smack little Brian,
no matter how much you might have wanted to,
because little Brian was stricken with vandalism,
and because little Brian didn't belong to you.

Sign of the Good Eye

Took a while, but I finally found someone
who would do it, who would make

a homemade sign for outside my door
that reads *no war or violence permitted in life*

which is the first sign that came to my mind
after the *no solicitors* sign we'd ordered came in.

Since that sign we asked for worked so well,
I figured it was worth a try to see how strong

a sign can be. How potent. *Magical*, even.
The next sign will say *no speeding at all ever*

anywhere in the world and I'll mount it right
below the other several signs by my door.

The change we want to see: two inches by
six inches of black plastic and mountable

with double-sided tape. Tape that clings firmly,
like I have been doing to some little hope.

the sea, unvisited

the cat, she's bathing by the window
fat calico jammed up onto the sill
as a passenger plane roars overhead
you just know someone's
on that plane in need
of a good shower

but then the microwave beeps,
you were using it for a timer
but what on earth for,
what were you trying to time,
what were you timing

and now your clothes
are clean but wrinkled

what distracted you

someone on the radio
mentions a thing about
provocation, a saber rattled
over a green sea you'll never visit
another voice is heard
chiming in that the Presidency
shouldn't normally be thought of
as an entry-level position

the calico is now around your feet
affection or alert or asking for something
and how long have you been standing still
in this kitchen

Something to Cry About

The house fire began to cry.
She had been working hard
on this home on the edge of town
for what seemed like all afternoon,
fully enjoying herself in her bliss,
this eager, smiling blaze she was,
and she was halfway through
consuming this residence
and now the fire department
had to show up and ruin everything,
just like they always did.

In a whirl of anguish and rage,
the house fire ran down the stairs
and met the firemen at the front door.
Why are you guys trying to put me out?
she sobbed, loud and desperate
and with a rush of red, bright air,
just leave me alone and go away
she screamed, she wept hot water
and her tears were fast embers.

She drew in a lungful of air
but then caught another scream
before it could leave her throat;
she knew it was useless to argue
or to beg these plastic men for her life;
she knew they didn't see her as worthy,
didn't see her the way they obviously saw
the ones just like themselves;
this was all the more frustrating
because the firemen *were* yelling,
but they were yelling at *each other*,
not at her; it was humiliating;
it was almost like they couldn't hear her
no matter how loud, how bright,
how hot she made herself.

The end arrived with a sound
like a seashore shushing you;
the firemen brought more water
than she was able to burn away;
the firemen all swore they heard screams, too,
but they never found a body.

Giving First Aid to the Scarecrow

Came home that afternoon, after work,
an hour after the punch of the clock,
after a long drive home.

Closed the door of my car behind me
as the cool Fall air embraced me
there in my driveway.

Saw my scarecrow, upright on my front lawn,
saw that he lost his left hand sometime between
this morning and my arrival home.

Had to give him some first aid, my scarecrow,
had to get some straw from the shed
so I could make him a brand new hand.

This is what fathers without children do.

Father's Whistler

They say that if you lose a tooth in your dream,
it means that someone you love will die very soon.
I never believed in that little bit of folk wisdom,
mostly because I was scared that dreams could really mean things
but also because I never cared for the hippie types
who helped to promulgate such bunk into the culture.
They say that if you lose a tooth in your dream
it means that sometime in the next week
one of your light bulbs is going to go out.
I dreamed that I lost a tooth only a few months
before we lost my father to the ravages of getting older;
I keep that tooth in a jar in the bottom of my dresser
to remember what it means to cage something important.
About two weeks after the funeral, I noticed that
I was starting to grow a new tooth in the hole
left behind by one of my wisdom tooth extractions;
I thought it was strange but I didn't dwell on it.
Another new tooth started growing right behind
that new wisdom tooth about a month later.
This kept happening and hasn't stopped happening;
I keep growing new teeth at least once a month.
It's got to the point where it's physically difficult
to spit out the phrase new teeth at least once a month
with all of these new teeth getting in the way.
I went to one of my dentists to discuss this freakish growth
and he told me that the new teeth were coming from my father;
my dentist told me that each time my deceased father
dreamed of me, from beyond the grave, in whatever bed
he may have been lying in out there in the next world,
a brand-new tooth would appear in my mouth.
The truth of this hit me quickly and instinctually,
thickening in the air like so much pungent incense.
As of the time of this writing, I can't sing anymore,
because I now have over one hundred and sixty teeth in my mouth
and the number keeps growing each month and week.
Truthfully, these new teeth prove that death has a beautiful smile,
though I would give anything to be able to whistle again
without sending sparks flying everywhere.
The thought of salt water taffy terrifies me.
If I could get the words out without screaming a song
about nails on a chalkboard, I'd tell you I miss my father.

An Apple A Day

His name was Dr. Jonathan Norquist, and he was my primary care physician. He was that until I did not want him to be that. Until I no longer felt safe with him doctoring me. I tried one day, after a handful of years of being under his care, to tell him that I no longer needed to see him. I told him so right in his office, at the conclusion of our last visit. At this news, he became visible. And he also became visibly upset. He told me that I "needed" to see him again, and I said no to him. I actually screamed it, and jumped off of the table that had the paper on it. I ran out of there, still just in my pale pink johnny gown, running for my life, across busy streets and buzzing front lawns, the hem of my gown trailing behind me in such a way that it made me look like an adult male little girl, and got home. Over the course of the next several days he or Kyle, his assistant, kept calling me and leaving me harassing messages talking about how I really needed to follow up with him. I didn't respond. Soon, Dr. Norquist started showing up at my house, looking into my kitchen, bathroom, living room and bedroom windows to see what I was doing. His eyes would grow wide at some of the private things that I would do. Being stared at through the window didn't bother me, but I was afraid that soon he was going to force himself into my home, and so I chose to remember the old proverb. And quite luckily, I had several apples on my kitchen counter during that time, and I placed one on the ground right in front of every possible way into the house. This worked like a charm; he couldn't get within even a foot's distance to the apple without suddenly seeming to experience a large amount of invisible pain, as though he'd become without warning the voodoo doll of some unseen child god. I'm very sure that doing this saved my life. The only catch to this solution is that when any of the apples start to spoil, I have to quickly run out of the back door and down to the supermarket down the street to buy more apples, and when I get back home I have to replace the apples really quickly, because I can actually see when the apples that are spoiling start to lose their effect on him. But you know what? He can growl and curse and grow a wild beard all he wants, and he does so constantly - I usually have to keep the radio or TV on real loud - but he's not getting in here.

Dat Ambulance

I try not to be angry
at the ambulance driver,
but I cannot help me.

I see the ambulance
careen down my street
going vroom so I boom.

The thing I think of in me
is how come I don't get to go that fast;
I imagination blow up that ambulance.

Dat ambulance.

The ambulance driver
makes a sudden noise in my life;
I don't like the sound
of the ambulance driver's existence.
The *weeeooo-weeeooo* is not a bird song
and I angry at the *weeeooo-weeeooo;*
I angry at it.

I imagination
a concrete ramp suddenly appearing
in the path of the speeding ambulance
and then the ambulance somersaulting in the air;
I imagination good.

I know the difference
between an ambulance and a fire engine;
an ambulance is white
and it has red stripes on it
and it contains a person who is crying.
A fire engine is big and red and it has silver on it
but I don't know what the people on it are saying.

I try not to be angry;
I try not to be angry at the person
who is carried inside of the ambulance
but the ambulance makes a noise
that makes me hear the color red too hard.
I imagination no more ambulances.

Got Me Some Brand-New Allergies

I thought about eating some peanuts,
and I woke up the next morning all swollen.
And now after that forever I wake up
completely swollen in the mirror.
This is how I became to have to live
with all of my allergies that almost kill me a lot.
I can't eat milk because my body will not tolerate
under any circumstances any milk. None. No.
My body is speciesist and ageist and also
alarmist and Sunkist against woke yolk
& intersectional, *dialectical* milk drinking.
It just won't have it. I can't have dangerous milk.
I had some milk on accident last morning
and as soon as I took a drink one of my eyes came out.
And then one of my feet turned into SpaghettiO's
and I coughed up a whole baby that was crying.
Milk is a bad thing for me, although they say it's from cows.
One time I ate some pizza that had an onion on it,
and I wound up in a wheelchair for the rest of my life
for several tragical weeks because no one believes me.
I'm allergic to other people who have allergies, too.
I mean, I'm allergic to them *having their own allergies*
that I don't agree with either religiously or dietarily.
There's a woman I know who is allergic to whey.
She says she can't have it. Like, *no whey.*
That's what she says, anyway. I always look at her
weird and give her the hard stare when she brings it up.
See, because I like eating things with whey in them,
it makes me sick to think of her not eating any whey.
I get hives and colors and all kinds of bumps
when I learn of another's allergy that I don't like.
When people have allergies I agree with, however,
I also get bumps and colors but the good kind.
One time a guy told me he was allergic to other people
breaking wind around him, and my body reacted positively,
including a baby's arm holding an apple springing
out of the front portion (or area) of my back.
Not to get into a *he said, she said* thing here,
But sometimes I look down at the front of my body
And I have to wonder what Mother Nature
Thinks she's trying to pull here.
I can't eat water. I'm able to drink it,
but I become allergic to water
 every time I try to be eating some of it.

So many people truly don't understand
that water isn't always a good thing
or something safe to be around.
I can't do almonds, also. I was given some almonds
by a very nice man with no name
and only a hazily-remembered face
when I was very little small, and it caused me
to break out in wheelchairs all over me.
It took days for all that to clear up.
Turns out I'm also allergic to being punched
in the mouth: that happened to me several months back
when I yelled at a boy who was taking too much time
at the salad bar, and as he hit me, my body started
acting allergically to his fist, with blood and teeth
coming out of my mouth and my lips.
It was painful, and I knew right away
that I was allergic to violence upon my person.
So if you see anyone moving fast and seeming like
they're about to punch me in the mouth,
please be ready to help me.

Every day, I wake up completely swollen,
thanks to how my body reacts to things.
Think about me in that situation:
all *swollen*, and needing help.

Maybe It's Time

Do you find it difficult to fall asleep, even after working all day?
If you answered yes to any of the questions above,
maybe it's time to ask your doctor about *Solacta,*
the only pill for anxiety relief clinically proven not to come in a pastel color.
Some subjects in recent clinical tests reported brief bouts of screaming,
yawning, and, on one memorable occasion,
screaming and yawning at the same time.

Do you constantly feel as though the pressure is mounting on you to succeed?
Do day-to-day chores fill you with dread and longing,
causing you to stare out the window
in soft-focus slow-motion at the end of this ad?

If you answered yes to any of the questions above,
or even if you didn't, and are simply curious
about what sorts of super-powers you can get,
maybe it's time to ask your doctor about *Solactaphil,*
the only nervous condition pill that actually sprouts two hands
and gives you a shiatsu massage and sings to you.
The most common side effects with *Solactaphil,* include:
shortness of breath,
shortness of erectile function,
shortness with other people who didn't deserve it,
and shortness.

Does a simple bus ride fill you with unexplainable fears?
Do you burst into tears at unpredictable moments?
What about flames? Do you ever burst into flames?
Is the breakfast menu overwhelming?

If you're human, and within the sound of my voice,
maybe it's time to ask your doctor about *Solactaphilialasil,*
the fastest pain, paranoia and monster relief medicine
available both over the counter and through the woods.
You should not engage in any activity
after taking *Solactaphilialasil* that requires consciousness.
Peoples should oughta use extreme care when engaging in these activities
the morning after taking this shit.
Side effects may include unpleasant taste, unpleasant attitude,
pheasant attacks, headache, dizziness, drowsiness, epilepsy, exorcisms,
waking up in used car lots, candy addiction, visions of cardboard box forts,
beautiful French Ferris wheels, green clovers, pink hearts, yellow moons,
orange stars, blue diamonds, pornography and lightning.

Are you breathing?

Then, maybe it's time to ask your doctor about
Solactaphilialasilazonetinspeealadocious,
a difficult-to-pronounce but effective solution
to waking up and getting out of bed.
Warning: mispronunciation of this medication may result in sterility,
mental telepathy, obscene wealth, poverty, invisible obesity,
and the power to command the snakes.

Ok, maybe, just maybe,
it's time to ask your doctor *what the fuck;*
what in the hell is happening to all of us
now that we need glow-in-the-dark green butterflies
sneaking in through the bedroom window to help us sleep and dream.

I'll tell you what: I'm gonna ask your doctor
how it is that whole generations of inventors and astronomers,
great thinkers and achievers,
the civilization-builders who came before us
managed to cope with the million cruelties life sends along
and still build this big, beautiful world we seem so afraid of today.

How far backwards have we run?

Ask your wise man if the wheel is right for you.

There is Fruit in the Garden Here

All of the signs pointing the way to your survival are right there in front of your eyes, if you will only look for them. Conversely, if you don't look for these signs, then they will point the way to your destruction. For example, there is a sign scratched into the tree by the general store that means *leave quickly; a judge lives here*; you have to see the tree in exactly the right afternoon light to notice it. Another sign is carved into the back of the Wilkinson's barn; this one means *a brutal man lives here, tell him you were in the Army.* You'll know this sign because it resembles a letter Z inside of a box. Continuing along, you will see that there are two signs scrawled onto the wall in the cellar of McGillicuddy's Saloon; one means *a doctor will take care of you for free here*; the other sign means that *everyone here will tell you to go to Hell,* with the possible exception of the doctor, who, as the sign says, will give you medical care for free. It will take courage to recognize these signs for what they are, and it will take strength to do as they tell you. The rains will fall on you as hard as they fall on everyone else, no matter how hard you pray; all the signs pointing the way to your survival are right there in front of your eyes. *There is fruit in the garden here.*

What Number Is Your Pain

My doctor's receptionist hands me the intake form. I sit down. I fill it out: What is your name. Are you sure this is your name. Why is this your name. Did anyone unknown to you give you this name. Why are you here. What hurts. Describe the pain. Why aren't you somewhere else. Briefly describe the pain. Describe the pain at length. Describe the pain using elaborate metaphor. Describe how long the pain lasts. Does the pain have any distinguishing features, like scars or tattoos. Are you sure you are in pain. Did anyone unknown to you give you this pain. Describe where on your body the pain resides. Does the pain reside there, or is it just visiting. Is anyone pressuring you to discuss this pain. Why are you in pain. Do you think you deserve this pain. Why do you think you don't deserve this pain. Would you like to nominate someone else to receive this pain. How come you're complaining about this pain. Forget about the fact that there are other people in the waiting room with you: what is so special about you that you think you should ask the doctor to take away this pain. You may either strongly agree or weakly disagree: do you smoke or do drugs or engage in sexual activity with more than ten brand new strangers in a month. Do you know anyone who does drugs or smokes or engages in sexual activity with more than ten brand new strangers in a month. If yes, please list the names and phone numbers of any people you know who smoke or do drugs or engage in sexual activity with more than ten brand new strangers in a month, and supply a ranking order of these people from the most attractive to the least attractive. Also indicate whether any of these people are into receptionists.

III.
Black Licorice Twist

The Sleep of Angels

When I was very little, perhaps a year old at the most, Jesus appeared to me in a vision, floating in a glowing gold dream bubble over my crib, and he allowed me to understand English so that I could understand the Good News that he had come to give to me. In my baby voice, I asked if he (Jesus) was God, and Jesus was all *I'm totally God, But I'm also me, and the Holy Spirit as well. Don't worry – not a lot of people get that.* Looking up at Jesus from my swaddling position in my pink and blue crib, I asked the Lord why he had come to see little old me. *I've come to tell you all about your mission in life – the one thing you were born for, the one thing you will truly be good at. I've got a busy day today, and you're the first on my list of people I have to float above and say special things at.* I asked Jesus to lay it on me. Jesus cleared his heavenly throat and began: *I say unto you that in your young adult life, you may have dreams of becoming all sorts of things in this world: you may dream of yourself as an astronaut, or a fireman, or a scientist or even an artist. But I'm here today to tell you that the one thing you will be good at in this life is eating pussy.* I swallowed hard and asked Jesus to repeat himself. *What I'm telling you is that you're probably going to be a schmuck at a lot of things in life, and you'll probably do okay job-wise, but what you're going to be legendary for is your ability and skill level at going down.* Nervous and honestly a bit bewildered, I pleaded with the Lord: but what if I want to be a scientist more than I want to go down? What if I don't WANT to go down? What if I turn out to be bad at it? Jesus took a pull off his beer, exhaled a plume of blue smoke and tapped his ash into the tray. *Little dude, I'm Jesus, okay? What I say goes. That's why I'm Jesus - I know shit and I foreTELL that shit. Trust me: you're going to want to, and the ladies are going to love your mouth, and you're going to love using it. No joke, my little bro, no joke.* And with that, the Lord disappeared in a heavenly cloud of mist, and little baby me, with all my future all laid out right there nice and easy, I slept the sleep of angels.

Gently Now, Gently, Gently
Into Your Black Tactical Duty Jacket,
Your Striped Plunge Bra with Cherry Charm

As I watch the police officer person
spray people with orange hurt spray,
I stand alone, to the side, on my own,
as my own personal savior and person
and I wonder how many protesters
use animal products on their sharp,
tight little college-attending bodies;
I wonder what sort of food fragments
remain in the pink, toothy radiator
of the police officer person's mouth;
I stand alone, to the side, all my own,
as my own personal savior and person
and I reach over to touch some of the
screaming, genital-having protesters;
I reach over and into the black shirt
of the aggressive police officer person
and work my fingers around his nipple;
I snatch apart both bra and boxer short;
I stand alone, to the side, on my own,
as my own personal savior and person
and I carefully violate the protesters
and the aggressive, orange police officer,
feeling the way of my fingers upon their
eyes, t-shirted breasts, mustache, baton;
I stand alone, to the side, on my own,
as my own personal savior and person
and I take some of the protesters
and I mix them together; I disrobe
the people with politics inside of them
and I make them lie upon each other
and I move them back and forth
on top of each other to see if I can make
some new people, some new protesters,
and I also rub the police officer
all over the protesters and I rub
some of them all over the police officer;
I want to see if I can make people
who are half-officer and half-protester;
I stand alone; to the side, on my own,
as my own personal savior and person
and I do not need a bank, or a protester,
or an orange, mustachioed police person.

How can I help the police officer
spray these yelling, tight-bodied people?
How can I help these yelling, tight bodies
to hurt the feelings of this police officer?
I am floating through all of them now;
I can see inside of the young protesters;
I can see the soulful, throbbing meat of the cop;
I touch all of them and I play with them;
I transcend political economics
and economic politics;
I enter the police officer
and the sign-waving woman;
I enter them and I change them
and then I leave the screaming scene,
having changed their bodies and worlds forever;
there is no revolution without transformation
and we all must play the roles we are given,
the roles that I give to we all.

Show Me Your Pink

She asks me if I want to see her pink.
I say *yes, please.*
Up until now she has only stripped down
to her black bra and panties.
She smiles at me, laughs at my smile,
presses her tits together for me
and then gets up off the bed
and disappears from the room,
leaving me staring at the webcam view
of her massive, dimly-lit and empty bed,
the red satin sheets and pillows
looking like a war just hit them,
and then I see her return into the frame
holding to her chest two halves
of a freshly cut pink grapefruit.
Do you like them, she asks, giggling
and holding the two halves up to the cam,
showing me the glistening coral flesh
within the two half-spheres,
*they were on sale at Albertson's
for ninety-nine cents a pound;
I bought a whole bunch of them today.
They are gorgeous*, I tell her,
*will you bring them closer to the cam
so I can see them a little bit better?*
I couldn't figure out what to do
with all of that excitement
I suddenly had in front of me.
I looked away from the computer
for what barely counted as a moment
to look out the window.
It was almost five-thirty in the morning.
Everything I knew about myself
was falling from the sky,
including the Moon.

Ode to a Grecian Yearn

In bustling, wine-scented Athens,
a young man peers into a storefront window
at a sea-green acoustic guitar on display.
This instrument, like a curvy woman, reclines
on the Renoir couch of the guitar stand
behind the dusty glass, before his crystal eyes,
and he wants to know the song of her mind
as well as any music that might come from her body,
but he does not have the necessary Euros
to spend an afternoon warm in her harmony,
or maybe even a night alone with her Eros
on some white stone balcony under a Moon,
and this want within him, this fluttering yearn
is beating against the silver bars of the cage of him;
there is a silence inside of all the noise on the street
as loud as his racing heartbeat in this moment
and need is the only thing that he can hear.

Shooting the Breeze

"I like Dorothy's spunk, her vim, her vigor,"
says the Cheshire Cat,
with more than a touch of envy,
"perhaps one day she and I shall meet."

"What is it about her vinegar
that you like so much?", asks the Scarecrow,
puzzling hard with his drawn-on brow.

""Vigor", you fool, I said, "vigor",
can't you understand the difference
between one word and another?";
replies the Cheshire Cat, now simply
a disembodied pair of shimmering jade eyes
in the air above the yellow brick road.

"I know when someone's being a complete tool
when they don't need to be, how about that?",
says the Scarecrow, suddenly breaking out of character
in lines fourteen and fifteen of the poem.

"I'm sorry; I forget myself sometimes;
I really wasn't trying to be a douche," says the Cheshire Cat,
genuinely reddening at his own arrogance,
"so, er, where were we? Ah, yes, I remember now:
have you ever had occasion to see Dorothy naked?"

A Very Hungry Girl

Goldilocks pushed herself away from the table,
letting out a loud, satisfied belch, a real foghorn,
bubbly and fragrant in the empty dining room
in the large, quiet house in the woods.
She looked out the window and saw the Sun
landing through the black and green thick of all the trees
and saw that the Sun was taking everything with it.
The window was open, and she could smell
the smoky scent of the night approaching slowly in the breeze.
She felt, for a moment, a little bit ashamed of herself.
Had she truly gorged herself so ravenously on the innocent?
What happened to her? Why was the Sun leaving?
Before this afternoon came around she used to think of herself
as an old woman existing within a young girl's body,
but now, after what she'd done, she felt young,
too young, unable to explain her actions,
if anyone nearby should have asked her.
With great resignation, a church bell rang from far away:
Goldilocks could hear it just fine though it made her a little sorry
to know that knowing that sound didn't change the fact of what she was.
The day was dead and night had come, and Goldilocks' shining scimitar
reflected only the candlelight now from where she'd propped the bloody thing
in the corner of the dining room as the dining room grew.
Goldilocks got up from the table; she had finished eating
the last of the three bears and had to loosen her dress.
She was so full in her belly; she felt the need to take off her shoes.
She wondered if the bears kept any beer or dessert in their refrigerator.

Live Nude Mercy

Maxine glistens in the silver light and slinks on ice,
glides down the stairs in her white lingerie
and shivers her way to the center of the stage;
the air around her hisses like angered air;
I sit with my beer and my eyes turn into telescopes,
erect and polished and focused so very tightly.
About twenty to thirty other guys watch, too,
and they are a colony of leaping apes braying
with bottles of Budweiser in front of them.
Maxine's hips metronome to the rock on the PA
and her white garters glow like bands of sunlight
striping her fit, sinewy thighs in the silly, Day-Glo gloom
of this here titty bar on the outskirts of East Bitch, Pa.
Outside, if we listen closely, we can all hear thunder
making its presence known above our parked cars;
we're locked onto Maxine's glittery cleavage, though,
and then that bra comes off and all of our skullcaps loosen;
the rumbling storm outside the bar listens to our cries
but doesn't change its mind, and rain comes down
as we rain cash onto the floor before Maxine's endless legs.
Our mouths are trying to fly to where she's grinding
when she reaches for her left nipple and tugs at it roughly,
tearing the flesh off her breasts to show us what's underneath,
now that she's bare, naked except for those acrylic heels;
she's showing us the rest of her, her heart, her lungs,
the trickling rivers of blood beneath her everything else,
the logical, red extension of what we came to see
and I'm wondering if I'm the only one who's noticed
what has ungodly ungodly begun to happen to us in here,
to her *up there*, and where is this new music coming from;
where on earth is this new music coming from?

Posing for My Master

Oh, hello, my dearest Government,
I am vigilant white shirt standing here
on the Dorothy wheat fields
of Elysian Revolutionaryness,
the ones with all the purple grain
in my office in this building of my house,
and I will but once speak my peace once,
and then my peace I will give to you.

I believe in the invincible price of freedom,
and also that the Statue of Liberty exists;
I believe in the fidgety P Diddy liturgy
of the American Thanksgiving word,
and in the power of search and seizure
and I, like you, too, pray that the Taliban
will always be the people who aren't me.
Therefore, TSA, *if that is your real name*,
before I take flight on your young, pretty airplane,
I willingly and humbly submit all of my body
to your special, laser-of-the-future photography
that gives me all the radiation my growing cells need,
in the very and same poignant way
that Dr. Bruce Banner was created.

Transportation Security Administration,
I only ask that you capture all of my beauty,
every moist, sun-kissed, aching, dewy inch,
every *every* of my only *only* in all of my *look at this*,
every silken, billowing-white-sheet covered place;
please, photograph me tenderly and slowly;
be sensitive, be the edge of a rose petal upon my nape;
be the *"shhhhhhhhh"* to my *"hmmmm, what's that?"*;
let your eyes be like hands that kiss my music into silence;
take very clear, up-close and detailed photographs of me
in all my blessed, hard, angular and muscley perfection;
capture how like two bowls of kittenish soul my eyes can seem;
mark these hands and feet that type manifestos about
how the night is like a country road and vice versa,
all of my body's charming hills and hairs,
the evidence of manhood between my nipples and chest,
the fleshy rise and promontory of my sexual cock,
the mischievous navel between my center of gravity,
become aware of how I am a man
with all your brave and sophisticate cameras;

see and portray for all the world
every one of my form's gentle and breathtaking curves,
so like sand dunes of muscle and finger,
the cleavage of my rippling, oily pectorals
as they shake and flex where I stand
above the summertime sprinkler;
not shooting all of this malleable and compliant skin
means that the terrorists will have had *epic win*;
focus on my wistful and pensive buttocks,
like two twin Volkswagens made of meat they are,
parked very close, so close to one another,
snap an artful shot, won't you please,
of every single hole that I have to offer,
my mouth, my ears, my outlet and escape hatch,
so like the open mouths of baby birds in a nest.

Make me your own,
and ask me in a whisper
how anyone could ever fly
without this.

I am ready to be the Leda
to your electronic Swan;
your aggression excites me so much
I will hand you my boarding pass with a smile.

And, oh, my beloved supervisors,
if you feel that you need more from me
than mere boudoir photography can give,
why then, please touch me in all of my places
until, hushed and sweaty, you are satisfied
that the truth is a secret safe in your hands;
take my *please-be-gentle* and be rough;
love me tough, give me the unbelievable pleasure,
give me the speaking-in-tongues in my throat;
use your lips and official mouth europeanly;
make me afraid of the dark once more
and get me all rigid; make me ready
to offer up my half of maybe a baby;
bring me to the verge of paradise
with the back of your gloved and dominant hand.

Anything you want me to do, I need to do,
whatever you want, whatever it takes
to help make this dangerous world a safer place to be.

Premium Baby

A lot of people have it bad when they're born. But I had it very bad. Very worse. And I had it badder than you; I had it a lot very worse than you. When we were younger, my generation and I, when we came out of our mothers, the doctors used to hold us up by gripping our hind feet together, holding us high in the air and smacking us on our asses so hard that we began to breathe. I'm told that doctors don't do that anymore; I'm not sure if this is true, and there is no way to know for sure. It was different when I was born. Things were different, life was different. The world had only been in full color for maybe a week. Doctors were harsher and meaner then; they smoked while they worked, and these doctors had no fear of us. When I was born and I exited my mother, the doctor grabbed me by my neck, lifting me up in the air, squeezing his fingers tightly; he drew back with his right arm and punched me across the nose as hard as he could. I only knew of a few million other guys that had that happen to them. What made matters worse in my case was that I was a *premium* baby. Maybe you don't know about this, but premium babies are called that because they're born very, very early, typically nine months earlier than the date of their own conception, and so they are very weak. I was a premium baby and needed help to get out of my mother. They had to give me a little wheelchair that they put inside of her that I could get on and they built a little handicap ramp that came out of my mother that I could use; all of this because I was a premium baby. But the wheelchair and the handicap ramp wound up not working because they couldn't unlock the wheels. So what they tried instead with me was to fasten a truck winch to one of the tables in the operating room, and they attached some twine to the winch and wrapped up my feet in the other end of the twine and used the winch to try to pull me out of my mother. But premium babies can be very nervous about seeing light for the first time, and as most of my body was being pulled out of my mother, they told me later on that my little premium baby hands grabbed on to my mother's nether lips and tried to hold on and not be pulled out all the way. Premium babies have very delicate sensibilities, and so, as one of the stories goes, after the doctor punched me, as soon as I could breathe, I bit him in the mouth. I punched him in the crotch. I boxed his ears. I brandished a sword I found in my mother and challenged him to a duel. There was an incident and the police had to be called. It was very hard to be a premium baby. It was very difficulty, extremely umber and troublesome. Babies who are born premium produce milk for their own mothers, but in my case the milk was soy, and my mother never took to it. She told me it wasn't delicious, and that I was a bad baby. I was a premium baby and I was a bad one. And now I'm just here, outside, in the cold air of the city, and I'm waiting for the city bus. I'm always waiting for the city bus. All of us who used to be premium babies, we have to wait for the city bus, and we have to wait forever.

Law and Order

The policemen, in riot gear and gas masks
and sexy, black flak jackets and boots,
work up one side and down the other
of the homeless man who was asking for help.
Their clubs against his body make a hot,
enticing Latin rhythm that I begin to dance to
right there on the sidewalk across the street.
Their clubs so sleek and smooth and shiny.
My hips move to the salsa, to the *grio picante*
of the insouciant percussion of their truncheons
on the skull of the desperate homeless man.
This hot dance music of punishment belies
the Chicagoish nature of this urban city.
The homeless man, with impeccable taste,
in muted hues of brown corduroy and tweed,
screams and yelps and squeals and honks
in time with the bossa nova swing beat
of the sticks that the cops rain down on him
like hard, dark, chocolate Kevlar kisses.
One strike to his face, one perfect scream
and the rhythm of the night will get you.
As the autumnal moonlight bathes the scene
in a phosphoretic, Hollywood white glow,
I run my hands over my chest and hips
and I lose myself in the dance to the rhythm,
the music of the status quo metro beatdown.
A little faster, please, I hiss breathlessly to the cop
who looks to be the leader of the squad,
a little faster please oh god I'm almost there.
I tell it to him through gritted teeth
and he looks at me, pauses with his stick
and then poses for me over the homeless man.
Me and the cop lock eyes; we're going to
have each other tonight and it's going to be hot.
The homeless man lifts up his head and
winks at me with his one remaining eye;
he gives me the thumbs up and licks his lips.
Passion is for the sexy people of the night,
he seems to say, gasping in his death throes.
I'm so ready now that it hurts in my panties.
It's time for me to get these wet clothes off.

Anchoress

Reaching gently into the screen
of her big, big Sylvania television set,
the woman wraps her fingers around the body
of the blonde morning show news anchoress.
The news anchoress screams,
but it sounds small in the living room,
door-creak tiny, given the difference in size
between the human woman
and the blonde morning show news anchoress.

Accompanied by a loud, short buzzing sound,
the woman pulls the blonde morning show news anchoress
through the soft glass of the television set's face;
the white cat on the couch, bored and detached,
observes and says nothing, despite the miracle in the den.

The woman pulls the blonde
morning show news anchoress
close to her face, inspecting her,
all the whole while not really seeming to hear
the news anchoress' screaming,
plucking at the anchoress' hair, curious.
The anchoress, who is blonde, and morning show,
is the news, while screaming for her life,
which is in the hands of the human woman.

The human woman slowly removes the clothing
of the tiny, panicking news anchoress.
The anchoress' news legs twitch and jerk like bug parts,
and her mouth becomes the lipstick gateway
between nightmare and the alarm clock sounding;
the human woman smirks, amused by the fear.

The white cat leaps from the couch
down the to the floor and out of the room,
seeking amusement elsewhere.

The woman and the news anchoress
are alone now, and can have their privacy.

This Is Happenstance

This moment here,
when I'm putting potatoes in a bag
in the produce section,
when I am another soul here
with a light above my head
looking for the scale
and I happen to look over,
see you looking at me
from behind your far-off shopping cart
with a salad mix in your hand,
you are leaning down a bit
setting your choice into the cart
and your blouse a bit open,
showing me the color of your skin
in the soft light of a glimpse;
my mouth opens a bit;
all you would have to do now
is walk over to me
and give me your number
on the back of a receipt
and we could be sweating the lipstick right off of you
your lips, a blurry little rose
in a room we go halfsies on;
any number of things could happen
if you could only see
this moment here
in the white business light
between us
just above the oranges.

Mary Kay Letourneau Cannot Sleep, Writes another Love Note to Vili

There's an odd stillness in the moment before I climb into bed with you, and then when I do the house spins and rises and journeys over and above the prairie, my love. You kiss me, and everything turns into a hard landing in a field in Oklahoma; you place your body with mine and all the world becomes a summer in Kansas. This merging of us, this making love, this doing it is dangerous; we fornicate with bleats and honks and our sweat becomes the mud that follows a beautifully disastrous rain. We know each other hard, *carnally*, making a change in the weather and as we do, the ceiling flies off of our house, yanked, snapping, from its moorings by the wind's strong, irresistible fingers. Our bed doesn't move, though; it is like a rock. The four walls of our bedroom fly away also, and we are on our bed in the middle of the quiet, Wild Plain. In our underwear, and then naked, and then the sky turns yellow and then dark yellow and then it turns dark dark *dark* as the storm of what we are creates a new weather all around us. As we ride each other, slick with sweat and singing with quickened breaths, the oppressiveness in the air forms a wicked, raucous cyclone of stormy black debris. Right above us, there's a circular opening in the center of the funnel, hundreds of feet around, reaching straight up for miles and the walls of this opening are made out of rotating clouds lit up brilliantly by constant flashes of lightning that zigzag from side to violet side. The sounds of indescribable screams fill the air; there are cars and horses flying around everywhere in the greenish-black sky above us and all around us as we writhe; people are running past us on our bed from every direction, bleeding, covered with mud, many with hardly any clothes on at all and finding it difficult to breathe, finding themselves lifted from the ground and crying for help around our bed. My darling, our sex rumbles into this town like a freight train, and when we're done the survivors all talk of how ominously we came, how suddenly we and our red silken sheets disappeared, whistling like ten thousand devils back up into the sky.

Pretty Dirty Vol. 5

These little sex fiends know exactly what they want,
said the DVD, and I glared at it, astonished;
there was so much bright, slippery pink in the pictures
I thought I was dreaming about Renoir's *shiny wet grapefruit* period.
I stood there in the adult video store, reddening,
wondering how those little sex fiends could be so young
and still know what they wanted out of their tiny lives
when Jesus didn't know his mission until he was thirty-three
and older in age than his own impossible father.
My grandmother, may Heaven rest her weary, doilied soul,
once whispered to me that God will not help you
find what you should want, that you should try to make
what you want fit into what God thinks are his desires,
so I suppose God already told those blushing little sex fiends
that they should want hotel nights that look a lot like
someone threw a bunch of flesh-coloured crayons into a blender,
that they should want a love that looks like a geyser made of milk
that lasts for four noisy, squishy, excruciating hours,
or eight, if you pressed play to play those girls again.
How could those little sex fiends have already decided
what they wanted out of all of the living of life
when Socrates, *for Christ's sake*, didn't even know what he wanted
until his slave-boy handed him an apple made out of hemlock?
With my heart, I think back now on the back of that DVD
and those soaking wet, oil-slickened human girls,
and I remember burying my mother, at her funeral,
the green grass a blinding, tear-inducing color in the Sun
and the shame of crying in the middle of the day,
wondering if I should have known by then
what I wanted my life to be and to consist of,
and never imagining that one day I would encounter
a handful of little sex fiends who already knew what they wanted
by the time I was old enough to be their unattractive President,
and how their surety, their confidence in their mouths and holes
would give me sufficient pause to question just how much
I know about what I want my life to resemble,
how much red, how much ochre I want in that picture.

**A Luscious Red Popsicle is Sucked Upon by a Luscious Model,
But I am a Good Person and Will Not Be Moved**

The young model sucks on the cherry orange popsicle,
pulling on it with her lips suggestively, as if to suggest
that she is truly blonde, and made perhaps of libertine, European stock,
open to the idea of a playful afternoon, and sexually creative.

Her dark blue eyes think dark blue notions in my direction,
staring into the camera while fellating the frozen treat almost whole
while I am the one standing here, leafing through this magazine,
passing the time until I must go to see my dentist.

Suddenly, I realize what the model is trying to do to me,
and I roar in lion-like defiance, right there by the pharmacist's window,
startling the baby in the shopping cart that happens to be passing by;
I cannot let myself be taken in by this supermodel's mouth.

You're not going to do this to me, I scream up to the heavens,
and I start to tear apart the magazine, even though I have not paid for it.
That's about enough of that; you better knock it off or I'll knock you out,
snarls the baby, pounding his fist into his hand and giving me the death glare.

You heard me, continues the baby, menacing me from his perch
on top of the shopping cart, *go ahead and keep it up if you want to die.*
I back away out of the store slowly, never taking my eyes off the baby,
our guns still trained on each other, neither one of us wanting to blink.

Holding You in the Light

Hey,

I want you to know that I know that you're going to be masturbating soon,
and I want to wish you every bit of success that you deserve in that endeavor;
I know you've worked hard for this opportunity, and I applaud you.

I hope that when you are masturbating you get everything you have been hoping
for, and I hope that fortune smiles on you as your little death makes you smile.

I hope that your bed is comfortable, and that the sheets are clean,
And I hope that no interruptions will emergency their way into your pleasure;
I hope sensual sounds will exit you like lithe young music slithering from a
saxophone.

I hope that you have all the toys and lube and heat that you might need,
and I hope that your imagination is a glistening elevator taking you to level one-
oh-one.

Knowing that you're going to be using your hands and fingers on yourself,
I'm holding you in the light; I'm holding you in the softcore porn light of hope;
I'm holding you in the xtube youporn light of redtube xhamster.

I'm holding you in the red light; I'm holding you in the 1980's pink light,
the grapefruit light, the banana light, the energy-efficient LED light,
the Jesus light, the Jesus-as-voyeur light, the God light,
the Heaven light, the Heaven of white lingerie.

I'm holding myself, also, in case you wanted to know.

And Then the Following Happened

I drank the exotic beer
and then a hot German girl
with milky, pale skin and big ones appeared,
and then after that
I ate the cat food and
then a meadow appeared
festooned with hundreds of animated fish,
and then after that
I brushed my teeth
with the new toothpaste
and then a photogenic version
of my wife appeared in the mirror;
we were both wearing white terry robes, Terry,
and then after that
I had some of that cereal
made from the fruit of the bran tree
and I smiled at the home breakfast table,
ready to face the day and happy in the knowledge
that I would be regular again
and that my ass would be happy,
and then after that
I bought the digital TV subscription
and right when I got off the telephone suddenly
I had four regular guy friends, all of us watching a football game
while a wife of mine brought in some buffalo wings to eat,
smiling behind her bright red crimson ball gag
and then after that
something must have been in that beer,
because after that
I shouldn't have eaten the cat food,
because after that
and right before I blacked out
I remember hurting some people
who were watching the game with me:

I pushed John into an open daiquiri maker
there was so much screaming
I must have lost control
people were yelling at me to stop

someone threw a dog at me

And You Were There, And Kierkegaard Was There,
And It Was Raining But It Turned Out That The Rain Was Wine

You could be the one
to make my dream come true.

All that you would have to do
to accomplish what no one before you ever could
is 1., have skin that's kind of a rubbery silver, and 2.,
meet me by the giant Olympic-sized swimming pool,
that one pool that's the size of about a hundred Olympic pools,
and then, take my hand and run with me
as policemen who are actually enraged, small-town chipmunks
wearing policemen uniforms
chase us off the campus of the Heathfield College for Advanced Psychological
        Studies,
where a conversation between me and one of the department heads
did not go so well because he tricked me
using psychology-based conversation tricks
into confessing my one secret shame
that I would never tell anybody,
no matter how close they got to me,
and in a panic I grabbed a brandy snifter
that was on his desk and smacked him in the face with it,
only it turned out I was stronger than I thought
and my smack caused his brains to go flying out of the back of his head,
which is kind of ironic when you think about it,
since he talked all smoothly and Freudly at me
and caused me to tell him all about myself,
while I had to use brute force
and all that got me was his moist, gray-green mind
splattered all over his library.

I know it's late, but please come on over;
I don't want to be alone.
I really think you could be the one
who makes my dream come true.

My Heart Goes Out to You

Sometimes the words we say to each other
have a tendency to float in the air
between us like a bright blue neon outline of a dove,
hung up there and held in place by nothing.

Sometimes I say what I mean to you,
and sometimes, what I say to you means more
than just the words that escape my mouth.

Take all the times when I say
my heart goes out to you,
for example.

When I say *my heart goes out to you,*
I mean more than just that I can sympathize
with the wounded and frightened fox of your emotions;
I also mean *my heart goes out to you* literally:
my heart goes out to you; it really does.
It goes out of my chest, softly, with no loss of blood;
it uses its little claws to push open the chalky,
creaking saloon doors of my ribs and it keeps going,
pushing through the skin of my chest
without tearing it or cutting me up like an art project
and it flies slowly forward and away from me,
out to you, out into whatever room I'm standing in
and then it goes through the doors of this house
and it flies slowly over the gray, motionless sidewalk,
stops at the 7-Eleven for a quick cup of coffee to keep it up,
pays the guy behind the counter with exact change
and it keeps going, my heart, as it goes out to you;
it keeps going; it stops to get a check-up at the doctor's office
at the bustling, busy corner of Wyoming and Constitution Ave
so it can know for sure it'll be strong enough to have you,
and the doctor listens through a stethoscope so freezing cold
I go *ahhhhhhhhhhhhhhhhhh* right where I am,
still by myself without my heart here in this house,
and then the doctor gives a toothy, thumbs-up grin,
gives my heart a little lime lollipop
and sends it on its way again,
and then, while it's still on its way out to you,
my heart takes a few rides on the roller coaster at the park
because it got distracted for a half a second and forgot where it was going
but that was only momentary and everything's okay,
and it's still on its way, going out to you now, my heart,

going far, going all the way through the town,
wearing an appropriately-sized helmet and obeying all the rules of the road,
stopping when the funny little traffic cop whistles
and going again when the whistling is done, going, going,
gone over a bridge and then through some piney woods
leaving cinnamon-scented, dark red contrails
in the heat mirage wake of its slow, bumblebee-like flight
and it hopes, it hopes that when it gets you
you'll hold out your hands with love in your blood
and carefully catch it between your palms,
let it flutter its wings and fold them in;
let it settle into place and trust your smell;
that's *me* you've caught in your hands there.

Careful now.

Don't make any sudden moves.

My heart goes out to you.

Be careful

All Natural

A church bell sounds metal and rings a mile away;
in the mood for communion I'm standing alone,
my flannel shirt unbuttoning in the piney forest
of Jaramillo, Texas early in the morning of a July.
I spy a cricket listening to me over the distant ridge;
I am one with the topsoil and hard stones under my toes;
I know the mission of every mammal and bird
that flutters and squeaks amid the pitch-black green
of this woodsy, natural and tree-having area.
This means I can hear the whispers of the feral
and I can whisper back; snakes slither past me.
One snake stays close by, pale and irascible *Naja*,
indigenous and natural to the wilds of Texas;
he watches me and knows that I belong here.
Not far off from where I am I can hear a wild boar
frolic with the rainbow carp in a watery river stream.
The leaves are afraid of the wind; that's the reason
they come up off the ground and turn around.
Notice my adequate heart and passionate equipment;
see how I can be green; notice how you can be pink.
As I unbuckle my belt and start to remove my jeans,
made from denim and as blue as a sky somewhere,
I smell the eucalyptus in the breeze between my thighs;
I close my eyes and I sing to the world that I am nasty.

As prickly hornet butterflies dive and swoon
around my torso, love takes me over; I'm yanking
my striped tennis shoes and gym socks off of each foot;
a beaver fixes me with a stare from his comfy perch
atop a large boulder across from me in this clearing:
perhaps the rodent is reading my mind and can see
that I am thinking of my ancestors as I make myself naked.
Looking back into the eyes of the beaver, my thoughts
travel through the air from my human brow all the way
over to his brindled, cinnamon-soft, stuffed-animalish brow:
"*I am not here to hurt you; I am here to live and die;*
I am here to become one with your little dam-making spirit;
I am here to make myself betrothed to mother's nature."
A mongoose peers at my naked, unclothed genitals
from the safety of a high branch on a nearby pear tree.
My coin purse trembles; his whiskers twitch.
My excited eyes are babbling like giggling stars.
Another signal travels from my mind to my hands,
and in a flash, I hook my thumbs into the waistband

of my dark blue satin boxer briefs and pull them down,
exposing my unashamedness to the light and air.
Removing my sunglasses, it is done; I am nude.
Nude and nasty. One with the wild world.
"*Here I am*," I seem to say, "*really naked and nasty.*"

I try not to focus on how much clothes I don't have on
when the peacock, native to this part of the Texas,
tip-toe struts up behind me and my naked, naked form.
He only wants to greet me, and welcome me here
because he is the king of the dark green forest jungle
and he will brook no misbehavior during this ritual.
My bumcheeks shiver, a cautious drop of sweat
trails down from the nape of my neck down my spine;
this fear I feel is nearly sensual; it is not creepy;
the peacock is right behind me now in this nature.
Turning my head slightly and very slowly;
I'm trying to conceal my motions so he won't startle
but the peacock catches me trying to look at him
and he roars, angered, chastising me with warning.
Frozen, I freeze, fearful that this bird will break my ass;
I'm shocked to learn a peacock's shout of challenge
resembles exactly like a mother lion roaring in rage.
Maybe today made a mistake in giving me over
to the earthen spirits that are forest-dwelling;
perhaps it's true I have not prayed enough;
perhaps my mind; it is not clear;
perhaps the peacock and the beaver
and the innocent, fluttering hornet butterflies
are all reading my mind right now.

Maybe they know that I am nasty.

Divine By Accident

Fallen rock star in my adoring sight,
disgraced and gorgeous leader of my body politic
and my free world,
maybe this is a weakness of mine
but I love the way you make mistakes,
I love the way you drop the ball and botch exams;
that's nice; that's pretty sweet, actually, see,
there's just something in the way you do things wrong so right;
the right-hand side of my sky is all that's left;
you perpetrate vanity and pride in the first degree
and I cheer you on until my voice is gone;
I love the way you get so impossibly hostile
at the drop of your own pointed hat,
the way you can stop on some kind of emotional dime
and the way you're always stealing that dime from someone else's tip jar;
I love how you're always so ready to throw *down* every time you fuck *up*
and I love the way you later on gripe *Jesus,*
the way you afterwards rage *goddamit,*
the way you death-glare snarl at anyone who sees you fail;
cussword assassin and *ever-so-pretty backstabber,*
I love the way you forget where you put the keys
and then blame it on the humidity, or the economy, or me;
I love the way you love it when a stranger trips and falls,
how you chimpanzee glory in the mishap that scrapes someone else's knee;
I love the way you assume you know everything
and carry on like you're the only one in the know
even when you don't know the first thing
or the last thing or anything in between about it
and how sweet *it* is, the way you blow through red lights when you need to;
the way you leave your messes behind in restaurants
and flit away like people only imagined you were there;
I love the way your lips never say *thank you* or *please,*
the way you highway and roadside litter
even in the most Autumn of country lane Falls;
I love the way you throw your shade around in broad daylight,
so much darkness in your eyes I could be excused for
confusing you with a zombie;
I guess I'm in love with every blessed blemish blossoming your humanity;
it scares me how much I scare me when I think of how safe I am with you;
this is dread in full color and it frightens the fear right out of me.
Why? Because your love addicted me at the very first feel;
it's funny how I thought I was immune, thought I was faster
than the oncoming disaster attached to a valentine arrow
but your love, your love is a tanker of frozen oxygen

wrecking spectacular in the rush hour of all my thoughts
and it makes the six o'clock news of me, all the time;
you make me want everything you shouldn't give to me.
So go on, keep on bursting peoples' bubbles
and demolishing the dreams of strangers;
keep committing every exemplary sin
every cell in your skin was made for.
Why? Because even though I know better,
I still love all these things about you;
they prove you're picture-perfection manifest
in all your precious imperfections;
if you never committed any of these crimes
I think I would find you boring to the point of telethon tears,
and I'd never want to find you at all;
in your selfishness limitless you're marvelous;
in your arrogance unwavering you're beautiful;
in your utter contempt for all that society asks of you
you're a vision in a cracked mirror; statuesque in your lovely brutality;
every flaw you have is a facet in the hopeless diamond you are
and you are perfect.

Statesman-Like

Abraham Lincoln in a speedo.

Abraham Lincoln
in a navy blue cotton speedo,
the dark azure dune
of his bulge piquantly visible,
lying on white sheets with his arms
folded behind his head
with a playful, come-hither smile in his eyes.

Abraham Lincoln in white swim trunks
on a blanket at Waikiki Beach,
working suntan lotion into his chest,
his grey nipple hairs glinting silver in the light,
in the hot Pacific breeze.

Abraham Lincoln leaning
against the wall all romantic,
just inside the door as you come home,
wearing nothing but the rose
he has in his teeth, and that big hat.

Abraham Lincoln in a black silk robe,
standing by the candlelit Jacuzzi,
waiting for you, wanting you.
Abraham Lincoln raising his hips.

Abraham Lincoln pressing his body
to yours in the back seat.
Abraham Lincoln's tongue,
in extreme close-up,
wickedly licking a wet cherry,
then, a quick cut to his piercing blue eyes
looking at you, at your body.

Abraham Lincoln onstage
at the gentleman's club, on his hands and knees
in the lights and noise, arching his bony ass
to the beat of the rock music, the sequins
on his orange thong glittering in the light.

Try to relax.

The Blood is Dry on the Dials
of the Daiquiri Maker

After you stormed off last night,
with the bells on the front door
still ringing like they could be heard,
I went off to our bedroom
and checked our joint email account.

I don't know where you went, or are.
Don't know if you will come back.
That was one hell of a bloody row
we threw, right there in the kitchen.

But we got a few emails that say differently.

The situation in the Middle East
emailed us and said they watched our blowup live,
and that our shouting and picking at each other's soft spots
came off as stale, weak, *phoned-in*, even.

The leaked photographs
of the naked and pregnant
twentysomething celebrity
found our camera angles too jittery,
the view of our dust-up claustrophobic.

The shoving match at the Lakers game
found our tears unconvincing.

Please come back
so we can fight again,
one more time in our kitchen;
the glass has been swept up;
the blood is dry on the dials
of the daiquiri maker;
I know we can do better than this.

Just Put It Out Of Your Mind

I'm doing everything I can now,
everything I know how,
everything I've been taught,
using all my strength
to not be thinking about Oscar the Grouch
in a moment of his sex ecstasy,
head thrown back, eyes fluttering,
mouth slightly, partially open
in the green grimace of his bliss
but it's no use, since you brought it up
I'm helpless now, hostage to my imagination
and the images come into being
like Polaroids healing themselves
after burning, glossy again
after surviving a house fire in a box;
I try not to think about it:
Oscar the Grouch half-sighing, half-moaning,
the long "oh god, please" hiss of his breath,
the "*ahhhhhhhh*" leaving his lungs
like entry into heaven was only this;
I picture him running his puppet fingers
through his short, rag-green fur
as his barely-existing hips lift up off the bed;
I cannot stop this movie, now that you've done this,
now that you have loaded this reel;
I watch his big, bushy brown eyebrows
lift up and then crease down as he rocks in his passion;
I see his stringy, pipe-cleaner-and-fleece arms
twitching, reaching up towards the ceiling fan,
the ceiling fan like the lashed eye of a god
that does not want to be seeing any of this;
Oscar the Grouch doesn't have any teeth,
so when I visualize him grimacing in pleasure,
and throwing his mouth wide open,
there's no tortured smile, just a wide, football-shaped hole
where teeth would be if he was human
but still had a head shaped like that;
I can almost see his God-strings
when he flattens his feet on the bed
and brings up his knees; he's whispering
to someone that he loves trash; he loves it;
I want to stop seeing these things
but my imagination is so strong:
damn you for wondering aloud,

when we were together that afternoon,
if Oscar ever had any lovers
and if his voice was that grating
when he moaned, when he came;
oh god, I am hearing him call *my* name;
he is pleading with me; this isn't right;
there are things we should not do;
damn you for this;
damn you.

IV.
White Chocolate

The Only One Who Gets You

This is the blueberry pie you were born to eat.
The blueberry pie that knew you as a child,
when it was just a blueberry pie child itself.
Do you remember? Do you remember the songs?
You and this blueberry pie once ran together as children
through sepia wheat fields, getting freckles at the same age,
all the magic of youngness long gone now.
There's a Don Henley song about it playing somewhere.
Oh, God, this blueberry pie, like ten thousand souls on a silvery bone boat
rolling over the moonlit sea monster waves of Earth primordial.
It has been waiting for you, here, under this glass counter, for thirty-two years.
And now this pie is looking up at you, locking eyes with you.
It is making little snorting noises in your direction.
On the shiny, aluminum platter under the glass,
the blueberry pie is vibrating, twitching,
pulsing and glowing as it watches you, tracks your every move.
Drop your bags. Get on your knees and press your hands to the glass.
Do not make kissy faces at the pie unless you mean to bury your face in it.
Put 'em on da glass, these emotions you have about pie.
Be free enough to cry if you want to; this pastry is now your mate.
Finally, your loved one. Finally, the one who could be your only.
Finally, your pie, this blueberry pie that will understand you
and maybe, if fortune allows, give you children.
Polite blue children with graham cracker eyes.
Grind your open mouth against the glass food enclosure;
get in the way of the other customers in line;
make them walk around the growling spectacle of you.
The blueberry pie is showing you its cleavage;
it is leaning down to pick up a napkin lewdly,
knowing full well you're taking in the sight of its surreptitious breasts.
This blueberry pie somehow already has your phone number,
and already knows the special way to bring you your private bliss.
Stare hard at the blueberry pie; make it know that you know
it's been watching you; bump and grind in the lunch hour.
Pay no mind to the other customers; let the world slip away.
The other people here don't know about pie, to Hell with them
and their indecipherable, crazy, non-pie-wanting ways.
Tear open your shirt and gnash your rapture teeth in the diner.
Wail at a religious volume; make a scene with your flaky crust.
You have found your dessert and you are justified.
Just a half-inch pane of glass between you and what you must have.

Between you and the end of the only pain in your heart,
your indigo heart that used to be strong sangria,
covered in a lovely purple goop now, your heart,
because of this.

Buy Some God-Damned Gold
(Everything I Ever Needed To Know About Paranoia
I Learned From AM Talk Radio)

You need to buy some gold right now.
You need to drop what you're doing
and buy some gold real quick
by calling this number immediately.
Men, you need to gather your women
and children right now, and place them
all around the hearth of your house
while you make the most important phone call you'll ever make.
Ladies, you need to put down your babies and aprons,
voter registrations and receptionist pencils
and you need to please pick up right now
the most important telephone you've ever known
and call this number right this second.

Gold is waiting for you,
and it's not going to come around
here at a price like this again,
not until the Moon is a tangerine claw
looming in the Eastern sky,
up in the eighth house in the year of the dollar.
The end of the world is a black horse galloping fast
and not no one not knows not the day nor not the hour,
so all of you listening to this message
need to stop what you're doing,
even if all of you are doctors operating on a person,
and call this number now so you can
buy all of this gold that you need to buy.
You need to buy gold now because the stock market
is not going to be in our lives here forever,
and neither will all of us be here forever in our lives.

Gold: it's the only way to bring God
back into our school and keep him in there.
With gold. With God and gold and golden god uniforms
for our precious baby children. With God and gold
go our golden, god-like children into the blessed afterlife
of golden hair and uniforms made out of Rapunzel-spun gold.
Please buy gold. Please? The boogeyman is coming.
Please, I'm asking you to stop being in your death bed
and crawl over to that telephone right now.
You can only get into Heaven if you buy this gold.
Please; this is the only thing that can heal you

if your inappropriate uncle touched you once.
Gold will cure all of the diseases that should be cured.
Women, please: gold. *Gold.* Don't stop.
Please buy gold now and put it inside of your bodies.
Between your breasts. Across your bums, please.
Please don't give your gold to bums, though.
This telephone number about gold
and how you can get some of it
is waiting for you so hard right now.
So hard. Oh, God, gold. Please.
The liberal hordes are coming for your gold
and you need to come, too, for your gold.
With Gold inside you, with God inside of you.
Please stop menstruating and call this number
that's all over your face right now
and have some of this delicious, salvific gold
up inside of you, up where we belong and where
the others who don't look like us don't belong.
Please buy gold right now by calling this golden,
shining telephone number right this second,
or the eye on top of the pyramid is going to kidnap your children
and kill them by stuffing them inside of a trash compactor
behind a building until they die by being killed.
The eye of the socialist pyramid, the socialist eye of the pyramid,
the one-eyed, socialist pyramid, the four-eyed, communist hexagon
is going to polio all of your babies if you don't gold;
buy some gold by gold calling this gold, golden telephone number
right golden now. Right now. You're going to die in a minute.
Please. Buy some god-damned gold. Now.
Pick up that gold-damned God telephone
and shower yourself with the richness of Gold this minute.
Please. Gold. Sexual noises.
Gold. Gold. Gold.
Ungh. Please. Don't stop.
Lord God Gold. Ungh.
Sexual gestures. Gold. Oh, Jesus!
Please, God: Gold.
Now, God. Yes, God. Gold.
Please. They're coming.
Please.
Save yourselves.

McDonald's Hiring Poster

In the first vision,
I see the McDonald's Hiring Poster
the way I first saw it in my life,
the way I first lived in 1986 in my life,
when I got that first job
just after high school and right before forever,
back in that manager's office
and there were nine of them,
nine free Americans all smiling at me
from just inside of that bright red and yellow poster.
Standing in tight 3 by 3 formation
and viewed from an angelic vantage point above them all,
they were every race and creed and sexual flavor,
all with the same exact *exact white teeth*,
African-Americans, white dudes and a winking pink dudette
and every shade of the rainbow
grinning together in name-tagged, two-dimensional harmony,
gay straight elderly heavy-set nerdy tough and milk-fed
these stepford paragons gazed upon me lovingly
knowing that I was about to join *the greasy slavery*,
all nine of them looking at me
and I swore I saw them all licking their lips
as I waded slowly in, waded
until I was up to my chest in a swamp of cooking oil
and everything was *America*
and I had to smile because I had a Coke
and America coated me in a sheen of submission;
I was her boy.

In the second vision,
inspired by the lifetime experience
of serving the public
which has always meant serving the Devil
which has always meant minimum wage for maximum abuse
I see it: the McDonald's Hiring Poster
frighteningly, fearsomely out of the frantic dark,
harshly spot-lit on a musty cellar wall
in the swinging, off-kilter glare of my unsteady flashlight
as I run and then stop, whirl around,
panting and terrified in a most lost and very haunted house;
all nine multiracial and multi-sexual and multi-trans
candidates for fast food employment
lift their bowed heads and then their happy faces *change*,
morph into scowls; I see the eyes on all nine

hollow out in an instant, their glares
floating quickly and irrevocably straight for me
from the depths of their empty eye sockets.

In the third vision,
I see the McDonald's hiring poster
tumbling up in the dark of the night air,
aloft on a stinking, apocalyptic breeze,
half-crumpled, one corner ablaze
like I just missed whoever lit it with a lighter
and I can see the multi-hued and multi-identity
McDonald's employees:
the young African-American girl
the older white lady
the middle-aged guy whose ethnicity I can't know
the teen person who I think is trans
like it matters what I either think or guess anymore
and they are all, together, unlike any hiring poster
I have ever seen; they're not looking at me at all:
they don't care if I want the job or not;
they don't care if I get hired or not;
instead they are bickering and fighting with each other,
shoving and screaming into each other's faces
like as if as though just like they were at an American rally
that was held in America to talk about America,
just like America has become one big angry rally
and melting pot screaming match;
I can make out the legend
welcome to the team
at the headline at the top of the poster
as the flames burn on, eating up the people
who once smiled at me
because McDonald's once McDonalded them
into whole, actualized contributors
to the economy.

In the fourth vision,
I see the McDonald's hiring poster
years and years and uncountable years
after the presidency of the Monster,
after America switched back to black and white,
after decades and decades of nuanced full-color,
after the end of the era of facts and truth;
I see the McDonald's hiring poster,
faded to a quiet, mere pastel of its former dayglo,
dilapidated, only three rusted staples fixing it

steady to a billboard outside in the rain,
the rain making every face on that hiring poster cry;
all nine prospective McDonald's team members weep,
wail and moan from the confines of the poster;
some of them reach to cover their mouths
to stop the sobbing
at the same time that I do;
why do these visions come to me now,
why do these visions come at all,
how many more will there be,
and what do they mean?

Who is the person
who can explain,
who can answer?

I love you McDonald's

I love you, McDonald's
I love you when you are eaten by me in the hospital
I love you, McDonald's
you never die or be angry with me
or be a father who doesn't know how to love me
I love you, McDonald's
you never be a mother so mean to me
and make me cry while learning to tie my shoes
you be French fries forever until my mouth
is a place i call heaven
until my mouth is in heaven
you be shakes you be shakes you be shakes
you be chocolate shakes
you be shamrock shakes that I remember when
they used to be pistachio instead of mint
you be the things my mouth remembers
I love you, McDonald's
don't you never be a cop made out of pepper spray
or an accident made out of ground-up people
I love you, McDonald's
and I don't care about life anymore, only you
I don't care who knows it
I need you in my bypass
I need the meat of you in me
I need your chargrill and your sauce
come away with me, McDonald's,
we will have a gay, beautiful, straight, heterosexual love
from which we can sprout children who have sesame-seed skin
I love you kind of like how I love
my bad uncle who's not allowed to see me anymore
oh McDonald's you are so hot I love you
show it to me
show it to me, McDonald's
take it out I want to see it
oh my God, McDonald's, it's so big
I love you , McDonald's
I love you when you be grease I can sink my teeth into
until i drown in pickles and brown cum
until I'm crying with my mouth full of breast
until I'm crying so much that my crazy me inside of me starts laughing
until I'm breathing cheese in a McEpiphany, unafraid of doom
please McDonald's I love you don't leave me
I drowned them for you

The Last Hamburger Speaks

I am the very last hamburger that no one ate,
still here at the end of the McDonald's work shift today.
It's night, and it's very late, and no one has eaten me.

I watched all day long, from my perch on the silver shelf
as one by one, my paper-wrapped brethren were bought,
and I knew in my heart that they were going to be eaten.

Every time I watched the slaves reach for one
of my people, one of my fellow hamburgers,
a tear would roll down the front of my hamburger face.

There isn't anyone at all who wanted to eat me today,
and no one wanted to eat me yesterday also,
and no one wanted to eat me the day before that.

All I have ever wanted ever since the day I was cooked
was for someone to come along and rip me apart with his mouth
as I watched him lick my guts and sauces off his fingers.

All I've ever wanted to do was scream as someone
ate me alive in several hearty bites; *what is the point
in living at all if I can't make a stranger's mouth water?*

I've thought about killing myself, about hurling my body
off this silver shelf thing onto the greasy floor of my world;
I know how a fall from this height would mean my squishy death.

The night has grown late and I can hear the spirits of the dead
as they float through the vaulted marble halls of this McDonald's
while the owls in the distant meadow screech in fear of the Reaper.

There is no love for me in this world; no one wanted to eat me
and bite through me and swallow me and digest me and pass me.
I wish I had arms so that I could cut myself, cut my own patty.

My buns are salty now, soaked down through to the pickle
with my tears, with angst, suicidal ideation and special sauce.
No one has eaten me, and, if I could, I'd end it all and eat myself.

So Damned Packed With Peanuts, Caramel, Nougat and Milk Chocolate, This Candy Bar is Literally and Actually Better than God

Delicious brown confectionate

you used your display at the store
to let me know

you would handle my hunger
so that I could handle anything

I listened to you, the way my ears
listen to the whining seagulls

I need to tell you something important,
you scrumptious, hot, two point seven ounces of candy

listen up

the police just came to my house
to tell me that my whole family died

they died in a terrible train accident this afternoon
as they were traveling across the country
to come and see me and visit for a while

and I don't even feel like I mind at all

because every time I clamp my teeth around you
I get completely filled up

with your nougat, your nuts, your caramel

your milk chocolate

it's like I never even had a family to begin with

No Other Men's Clear Gel Deodorant Is Stronger, by God

Relax; keep your cool in any situation;
Gillette's Clear Gel Arctic Ice antiperspirant deodorant
ensures that you'll stay feeling fresh and feeling dry
no matter where you are, or what you're doing.
No other men's clear gel deodorant is stronger.
All-day protection from wetness and odor: *stay confident*.

No other men's clear gel is stronger. Sweet Lord.
Do you understand me? I'm dead serious here.
You could be blindfolded in a strange, hot room
while a smelly, lisping murderer whispers to you that
your loved ones will never see you again, but you'll also have
all-day protection from wetness and odor; *stay confident*.

Ride a wave of freshness; experience long-lasting protection
even as the fiendish, giggling, ski-masked deviant
spits on you and tightens the knots in the ropes
that hold you to the filthy bed up in his attic;
no matter where you are, or what you're doing,
you've got all-day protection from wetness and odor; *stay confident*.

As the monster pushes the bamboo under your fingernails,
understand that no other men's clear gel deodorant is stronger,
that no matter where you are, or what you're doing,
you'll stay fresh and feeling dry because Gillette provides
something no other men's deodorant or God can claim to give you:
all day protection from wetness and odor. *Stay confident*.

This could literally actually be the thirteenth year
that you have lived as a captive in an unfamiliar neighborhood,
hooded and malnourished in a covered-up chicken coop
in the dark back yard of some psychopath's home;
relax and keep your cool in any situation; Gillette provides
all day protection from wetness and odor; *stay confident*.

Relax, you will be remembered as someone
who was always confident and kept their cool in any situation.

Jell-O Be

When I found out how they made Jell-O,
I was completely taken aback.
First, these five guys in white lab coats,
hollering and struggling and yelling,
have to figure out a way to cram a live zebra,
struggling and yelling also, into a drink mix blender.
Not as easy as you might think.
And this is an adult zebra, a grown one,
a zebra that can legally smoke and vote.
Normally, they don't even bother
to get the zebra's name, which shocks me.
After the men in the coats have managed
to get the zebra all the way into the blender,
they need to add more animals and flavoring.
They shove and push to get the pony in there,
also the octopus, tabby and crested grebe.
Once every animal is crammed into the blender,
it's time to start adding sugar and dopamine.
This takes a lot of stamina and much time,
as each five-hundred-gallon drum of sugar
must be hoisted up and above the blender
individually, by just one of the men,
while all of the other men must stand around.
Under any other circumstances, it would be okay
to help someone lift up a chemical drum so heavy,
but the Jell-O recipe is very specific about this
and must be adhered to, no matter what happens.
Once the sugar has been added to the blender,
the remaining men must then add the body
of the guy who had to lift the sugar into the mix,
because he died, so...
Many times, the guy who added the sugar
is put into the blender with his pen still in his coat;
this is how we get flavors like blueberry.
This whole process is a very careful, nervous task
that requires experience and faith, and magic.
And electricity. And a large platform near a ladder.
And light in the room. There must be light in the room.
A lot of things and animals need to be added
to make this happen, to make Jell-O be.

Capiche?

You'll rave to your friends about our
delicious, toasted sandwiches
here at Joe Friendly's Sandwich Shop;

you'll tell everyone you know
to go to Joe Friendly's Sandwich Shop
for the best lunch in town;

actually, you won't stop talking about
the incredible, affordable meal
you had at Joe Friendly's Sandwich Shop;

you won't if you know what's good for you.
If you have any smarts at all, in fact,
you'll do the right thing here and tell people.

You'll tell all your friends about our food,
and your family doesn't lose anyone else;
that's how this is going to go down, see:

you'll rave to all your friends about our
delicious and freshly-toasted sandwiches
here at Joe Friendly's Sandwich Shop,

and then? Then, no one else has to die.
We can end all this right here and now.
We've got the best lunch in town...*right?*

Nod your head twice for "yes"
if you understand what I'm telling you.

**On Witnessing An Instance of Magick Being Practiced
In a Walmart Parking Lot in Providence, Rhode Island
And Wondering If It Is Up To Me To Decide
What Means Something And What Means Nothing**

I was coming out of the Walmart
when I spied a real and skinny young man
with a very old and full long beard
wearing a dirty, navy-blue Adidas hoodie
(the kind with the many white zippers)
seeming to be praying or yelling by himself,
or maybe he was yelling prayers,
right next to the cart corral
where I was bringing my cart
after my prolonged bout of shopping.
Worried that his mentalness was a danger to me,
I slowed down and looked all around me,
scanning my surroundings for another corral
but the next nearest one was full,
and as I turned again towards where
the young man was busy shrieking to the sky
I noticed it sounded like he was invoking
a long serious of powerful-sounding names,
none of which to me seemed especially English.
His voice rose and I saw other people staring.
One heavy lady stared at me like this whole thing
was all my fault and we glared at each other hard
for a few tense moments, neither of us making a move.
The yelling man had spit flying out of his shouting mouth
and then I thought I heard the word *invisible*
and he suddenly disappeared from view.
He vanished right in front of us all, everybody,
but we knew he was still there
because he was now laughing as well as shouting.
So weird to hear laughter but not see anybody, right?
A Mexican woman near me fell to her knees in tears and
started praying loudly to God while sobbing obnoxiously.
Lots of the word *Dios* over and over again and then
I heard the sound of several men shouting with their afraid voices
and someone right behind me screamed *where's your phone?!*
and I thought a late afternoon in August was a bit too early
for midnight on October 31st to already be here.

Why couldn't I move at all.

My ice cream was melting in the bag
and I couldn't move at all for what felt like
a terrifying, eternal half hour.

Let Me Out

There's so much red in all the Target stores and I don't understand it. What are they trying to *do* to people? I'm sorry about yesterday; I'm sorry I told you that I didn't like you anymore and that I wasn't going to split the cost of the snacks with you; it seems like every time I go into a Target I get really angry. Why do they have to fill the place with so much red color? Why do they want to do this to me? I don't even know why we were there and I don't know that anybody knows why they go there. I think we were there to either buy some ginger ale and a chair, or a picture frame, or you needed to get some tampons or I needed a video game and some aspirin or else we needed to buy the idea that our future was going to be ok or else we wanted to find out if it was possible to have church anywhere or else have some dessert or else *hold me now* but all I could see was red. That bright angry red that says *you're not leaving here until you buy some electronics and Milano cookies*. That sweating tomato on the vine, shaking and about to burst like a throbbing brain, those holly berries like little crazy eyes. They make me think I'm capable of terrible things. Those red stone spheres in front of the Target give me the bad dream feeling that I'm going to lose control and become the first man who ever lived and donkey-punch someone's grandmother on the stairs, chainsaw everything in half. Every other breath I take in that place is an exasperated sigh and I want to choke-slam an elderly greeter right into the wall. Target makes me feel like I'm about to learn how dangerous nature can be, in the way that cavemen found out which of the colored sweets were the deadly berries. I feel like I'm about to *be* the dangerous nature when I'm there. All of that murder everywhere, all of that Target welling up inside of me like bile. I feel like I'm about to dropkick the nearest dachshund into next week. I can see myself backing over a soccer mom with my car because I don't want to check the rear-view mirror for fear of seeing all of that exciting goddamned merchandise in my eyes. I can't believe how big my eyebrows are. All that bright emergency ambulance red in the signs over every aisle, all that infuriating red has become a pulse in my skull and I want to leap over the counter and go after that cashier with his stupid bloody shirt and his way-too-tight khakis. I can't stop thinking about it once I start. Am I in a Target now? Is that where I am? I need to get the hell out of here.

Fifty Cents

If you have some extra change
when you're done at the supermarket,
fifty cents will give you a minute to try and pick a good baby
out of the bright red and pink claw machine
situated between the video rental box and the change maker.

Inside the glass of the claw machine,
there's a huge pile of fresh, clean and naked babies;
it's a cacophony of crying and laughing,
gurgling and spitting up and cooing and burbling
in every shade of brown and pink;
a music box of warbling and wriggling and goo-goo'ing.

Pop two quarters into the credit slot
and grab the little joystick;
don't let that *"pop goes the weasel"* song
and all the flashing lights distract you;
maneuver the three-fingered claw
over the neck of the baby that you want;
watch the fingers clasp around the baby's neck;
hoist the baby up and try to beat the clock
as you inspect that dangling baby,
as that baby looks you in the eyes.
If you do not like this baby,
jiggle the joystick to make the baby fall back down
onto the pile of all the other babies
and start over quickly, before the time runs out;
look for a better baby in the pile.
If you get a good baby and the claw gets a good grip,
use the joystick to pull it over the hole
situated at the right, near corner of the console
and then release it; the baby will drop down
through a chute and into the hatch on the front of the machine
where you can collect it.

If it turns out that none of the babies look appealing to you,
just make the claw drop the baby and be on your way.
After all, you'll only be out fifty cents.
Just don't look back at the baby
pressing her hands to the glass
and watching you leave.

First Rich Corinthians (Chap.4, Vers.1)

Supposedly someone once said that
insanity is doing the same thing over and over again
and expecting different results or expecting the Spanish Inquisition
I can't remember which at this moment
and I'm told that evidently Einstein was the person who said that
but I think there's plenty of reason to doubt whether or not Einstein even *existed*
since we're now living in the Seventh Dimension
which is the dimension comprised of cosmic particles,
sentient tweets and alternative facts
and in this brand new and quite grand dimension
we are all held for ransomware
while the ubiquitous and militarized police
walk back to their cruisers to see if they can get authorization
and hydroplaning means to slide uncontrollably on the wet surface of a road
and I'm sliding uncontrollably on the surface of *the 24-hour news cycle*
and while a gargoyle is defined as
a grotesque carved human or animal face or figure,
projecting from the gutter of a building and typically acting as a spout
to carry water clear of a wall I am defined as
someone who is going to insanely continue to hope for a better day
which might mean that I need to get my head examined or unpacked
but that might just be me being ableist against myself
because I've evidently contracted United-States-flavored Stockholm Syndrome
and a melodrama
a melodrama
a melodrama
a melodrama
is *not* defined as *a mellow dream,*
is defined as *a sensational dramatic piece*
with exaggerated characters and exciting events
intended to appeal to the emotions
but I've only got so many emotions left to spare:
this is 2017
this is two-thousand-and-seventeen
this is the year of our overlord two-thousand-and-seventeen
and one definition of bondage is
the sexual practice that involves *the tying up or restraining of one partner*
and another definition of bondage is the state of *being someone else's slave*
and if the President is going to continue fucking us
while *coup d'etat'ing* us into a corner store
can we all at least ask for ball-gags to drown out our screams
and a theater is defined as
a building or outdoor area in which plays and other dramatic performances are
given

and every day we look around
and find that all the store fronts and school fronts
are just clapboard facades *with nothing behind them*
and I regret to inform you that this poem
is not allowing cameras in the room today
and you are not allowed to report on the things announced in this poem
and you are no longer permitted to take pictures of this poem
and this poem will only be available for a few minutes behind the bushes
at 1600 Pennsylvania Ave
and no recording devices are going to be allowed
and any questions about why this is happening will not be allowed
and subjugation is defined as
the action of bringing someone or something under domination or control
and some nights I wake up
to find Sean Spicer kneeling down beside my bed
his face only inches from mine
and he says *you better not say anything*
and cotton candy is defined as
a mass of fluffy spun sugar, *usually pink or white,*
wrapped around a stick or a paper cone
and I wish I *was* a mass of fluffy and spun sugar
instead of this mass of frustrated and confused human skin and blood cells
wondering where the hell all my votes went
and sometimes I feel *unusually pink and white*
and even though I do not believe in God
I'm told that God doesn't take offense to that
which is a good thing, a happy accident, a boon and a feather
because I'm feeling the need to open up The Book of Gibberish
and turn to Chapter Four, Verse One of *First Rich Corinthians;*
I'm feeling the need to holler and imprecate
until the all that lightning in the clouds tonight
stitches together some words that maybe I can live by
until such time as I've got nothing more to worry about.

Coralescence

In the current, escalating world situation,
in the global economic crisis that we face,
I pour some warm, delicious Hershey's chocolate syrup
onto my single scoop of pistachio ice cream,
luxury pistachio, and I sit beside the pool.
I let the sun shine on me, everywhere on me,
and not on the economic crisis people.

As the leaders of seven industrial countries
confer in the important United Nations New York building
on how to handle the ever-worsening situation in the Middle East,
I quietly take many of my clothes off;
I slip into my iridescent, metallic-green swim trunks
and slide my gentle body slowly into the night-cooled water of my pool.
The water is wet on my skin, and my skin is wettened by the water.

As officials in Georgia struggle to defend the actions
of Atlanta city police during the weekend convention,
which left six regular people dead and a nation in shock
over a viral video of police brutality gone wild,
I sip my virgin Long Island Iced Tea methodically,
look down at my own coralescent, sun-kissed, dewy lips
as they shine in the golden, wealthy afternoon of my Jacuzzi.

The Red Cross estimates that nearly half a million people
may die of starvation over the winter in Eritrea;
officials warn that if action from the U.S. is not swift,
if the U.S. drags its feet on a bill on the table that would call for houses,
millions more may needlessly perish in the elements;
what I love about Lady Gaga's music is that it makes me feel free
to just dance wherever I want, and the haters can just suck it.

Civil liberties of all kinds are now at unprecedented risk
in the wake of the aftermath of the consequences
of the effects of the results of the memories
of the terrorist event that people didn't live after
and I love the feeling of velvet on my bare skin at night;
I love the feeling of scented pleasure oils on my body;
the sensual thump of tricky music pounding on the stereo.

Danger and Excitement Everywhere

Let me be totally honest with you;
I feel bad for all the female, piranha fish mothers
who have to breastfeed their piranha children.

Such an unimaginable pain,
such an accurate, agonizing feast,
a mantis-green blur of breast and teeth;
it hurts me to imagine it
every single time I imagine it.

One of the medical facts
about piranha fish is that
you can't make jawbreakers
that piranha can't handle.
I'm not saying you shouldn't try;
it's just that there will be a lot of noise
with not a lot to show for it.

Piranha fish can be found in the Orinoco,
which is a gentle, considerate river
deeply located in the Amazon basin;
the Orinoco is also an Enya song,
and Enya is a deep and considerate
Irish New Age folk music sort of person,
but Enya is not like a piranha fish
as far as I'm aware of.

It is not known whether or not
a piranha fish can angrily devour
a helpless, living automobile whole
in a horrifying matter of seconds;
I mean, it *is* known, but I'm not willing
to go along with that kind of knowledge.
That kind of knowledge doesn't like my imagination,
which is fine with me because my imagination
doesn't like that kind of knowledge anyhow.

Here is a new medical fact about me:
on the grassy, html-green shores
of the burgeoning, liquid Africa river,
where the snowy egrets singingly
land upon warm, sand-colored sand
so they can catch their wriggling, wild prey
in the buzzing, natural Amazon morning,

I have never been there.

But I don't need to swim in a river
full of naturally-angry piranha
to know that the world can be a dangerous place;
I can go to a McDonald's restaurant
and see that for myself up close.

I'm going to tell you something now
and you should probably write this down
because I'm a pretty trustworthy person
with all of this new information that I'm making up:
mark my words, at the next stage of evolution,
which is probably going to happen in an hour or two,
piranha will develop the capability of flight.

It's a terrifying thought; I'll agree.
But it's too late now.
I've already thought of it.

I guess what I'm saying is: *be careful.*

Redeemer

One day, Mr. Chimpanzee,
someone will come to your cage at the zoo
with a heavy, worried set of keys in his hand;
he, he will be the one to free you,
but no, he will not be the one
who put you in your prison to begin with.
Save your rage for the one who locked you up.

You've had plenty of time to learn where he lives.
You've taken notes of how the humans
get from one place to the next.
You will be able to have your revenge.
Have mercy on the one who
comes to free you on that day.
It will be before noon on a Friday.
The chill in the breeze and the leaves,
all will scream to you of autumn, of Fall.

Have mercy, Mr. Chimpanzee.

Have mercy.

Crystal Ball for Sale

She said she'd bought her crystal ball
at a Filene's in Wilmington, Delaware
and that she bought it on clearance,
and so her prophecies could not be trusted
to be exactly one hundred percent accurate.
I sat with her, at her little shop
on the Main strip in Bridgeton, New Jersey
where I'd got lost trying to find a poetry reading,
where I'd given up after about three years
of driving around aimlessly, trying to find the place.
I saw the fuchsia neon hand in the window
and I knew by the sign that this was the only way
to make having come all the way out here
worth my time, worth the trip at all.
She shouted that her name was Anna
and I felt like I knew that already
because her name was on the door,
and then she told me in plain English
that if this thing was going to work,
I would need to come in, relax, clear my mind
and take off my shoes and sit with her on her couch.
She had way too much tea rose oil on
and I was starting to get lightheaded;
I found it was really hard to relax,
as my feet don't always smell so good.
I kept hoping her tea rose smell,
which was murdering me, honestly,
would mask the smell of my feet,
and the stress of hoping for that, I'm sure,
probably skewed the results as she made
a whole series of wacky, witchy gestures
all around the crystal ball on the table before us.
She told me that a life-changing event
was headed my way, within the next week.
That was as exact as she would get with me;
she didn't try to put any moves on me,
and I drove home through a long, loud rain
it was almost impossible to see through.

This morning, one week from our little meeting,
I woke up to discover that I have become a hermit crab.
You have no idea how hard it was to write all of this down.

If I'm Being Honest

Not to be mean, but you are *nightmarishly ugly*. The kind of ugly that can change a stranger's whole personality at a distance. I think about where your eyes are on your face in relation to where your nose is and I start to wretch from the beginning of time. The sight of you makes me make sounds only a dog should be able to make. Or a wolf. Or a wolf trying to get down a spoonful of body odor. My father used to tell me fairy tales about your face so that I would have an easier time going to sleep crying. I saw someone who looked like you on television and I charged the TV like a bull, ramming my head through the glass until nobody was born anymore. My mind tries to handle how hard you are to look at, and in the process I'm not okay anymore. A bouquet of gardenias grows out of the back of my head. My aunt slaps my mother, even though the both of them are dead. This isn't personal, it's just all about you and how every time I happen to see your face I hear the angry roar of a chainsaw and I almost throw up food I ate ten years ago. Norman Rockwell went through an experimental phase once and created a painting based on a close-up photo of a maggot barfing up baby food, and the look on the face of the first person to ever see that painting is what you look like. I'm that person every time I see you and I want to strangle Norman Rockwell so hard I can hear my own knuckles melting. Your face is like what happens when a pile of dog shit gets overwhelmed by the futility of it all and bursts into tears. The first time I saw a picture of you, I killed myself, but then I had to bring myself back to life so that I could try to warn everybody.

Stretches of Spain

Spain, you are the country of Spain,
and America, in all her opalescent majesty,
she weeps blinding, diamondish tears for you
because you, Spain, are a third-world poverty country
with wisps of UNICEF rice on your mouth.

America, and all of her people
inside of her, they have to take diet pills
so that they don't have to countenance
how desperate, how shabby you are, Spain.
Oh, Spain, you country without language or medicine,
America will sing for you on a charity recording
so that you can have shoes and stoves
and some new loaves of bread.
We remember accepting your gift
of the Statue of Liberty that one time,
though we wondered to ourselves
how on Earth you could possibly afford it.
 Spain, you hobble and straggle along
with no government or education,
no art or hygiene: we know this
because we sent you the buckets of water
and yet somehow you have
a primo seat at the NATO table.
Spain, you don't have trees or flowers
like pretty, fluorescent America does
and America, wearing a dress made out of fashion people,
cuts herself because she is depressed about
your ability to not have any progress or evolution.
Oh, Spain, oh, emaciated, lost and micro-chipped Spain,
your fallow boulevards are only a foot wide
and you don't know that the rest of the world exists.

Ability to make industry,
how come Spain doesn't have you
like muscular, sun-tanned America does?
I'm sorry, Spain, but roses will never leap red
from your so-called soil;
your windows will never bejewel
with the snowflake baubles of Winter;
the United States of American
has roses, snowflakes and liberty, though,
and you don't have anything, Spain.

Oh, Spain, I toss you a quarter and a nickel
as I pass your cardboard sign
held between your crossed, bulimic legs.
I turn around, Spain, I do,
and I drop some American soap
into your hat on my way to the opera,
where I shall drink icy cold, crisp Coca-Cola
and hold some free elections.

Spain, I have seen the commercials
with the Sarah McLachlan music
and the Red Cross trucks
that advertise your perilous situation.
You don't have doctors,
or the rubber gloves that they might wear.
You don't have airplanes,
or flight attendants that might
call those airplanes home.
You don't have Ferris wheels,
or the smiling children that might giggle
and teeter on those things on Ferris wheels
that are like chairs for Ferris wheels.

Pitiful, pitiful Spain, with your lint,
your black-and-white, hi-res famine,
your cataclysmic, overwhelming *litter problem*.

America will save you, Spain.
America knows you need help;
America will Christianly hand you a bowl
and a warm, heavy pea coat
to shield you from the harsh,
apathetic and knife-ish winds of life.

But until we get there, oh Spain—
you nation without roofs,
you country without telephones,
will you ever come around?
Will you ever put an end to the black apple of polio?
Will you ever have painters and science?
Will you ever discover fire?

George Washington Gave Birth to America

Very little is known about George Washington.

Basically, all we know about George Washington
is that he was the father of our country, and, as such,
did give birth to this great nation of ours, and so,
it is right and proper and citizenish that we,
as people, reflect on and commemorate
everything Washington went through
to make sure that America lived and existed.

George Washington gave actual birth to our country,
feet up in the stirrups, screaming for an epidural;
our nation's first president perspired like a mule
in his tricorn hat and brown wool breeches,
crying and pushing on the operating table,
trying through gritted teeth to get all of us out of him.

He was brave, the way he hissed and bore down
to move all us huddled masses deep inside of him
down through his tight birth canal and out into
the bright white lights of the delivery room;
the heart monitor in the room beeped like crazy
as Washington screamed and bled, and birthed us,
his white wig sliding off his sweat-soaked head
as we crowned and screamed our way into the new world.

As all of our heads exited the first president at the same time,
some Americans came out breech as well as head first,
and the people walking outside on the sidewalk
across from the hospital could hear George's screams
as the interns ran around and fumbled to get the episiotomy ready;
orderlies ran around playing bugle music and boiling
the bed sheets that Betty Crocker sewed for this occasion;
the powder from George Washington's wig
got into the obstetrician's eyes as he shouted *push*
and the president heaved, sobbing and grunting
as the buckles on his pointy shoes came loose
and we all tumbled out of him and landed, scrambling,
on the frigid, craggy shore of Plymouth Rock.

#NotAllCompanies

In the event that a separation
between you (*Applicant's Name*)
and the company (*Futility Unlimited, LLC*)
becomes necessary, you agree
to hold the company blameless.

You agree to hold the company,
and in return to let it hold you oh so close.

You agree to hold the company
while the company takes you roughly,
with no finesse but at least a thoughtful candle going,
while the company takes you the same way
every night, without even so much as a kiss on the neck;
you agree not to look into the company's eyes
while the company has its way with you.

You agree to hold the company
tight all night long until the company
gets hard, gets off, gets bored with you,
gets angry, gets defensive, gets threatening,
gets rid of you.

You agree to hold the company
while working the shaft and balls.

The company needs you,
so stop thinking about yourself all the time;
stop being a fucking *nag*

look:

you agreed to hold the company

you agreed

Course Correction

A laughing gull stalls in mid-flight over the Bosque,
falls in cardiac arrest down to the wet earth
on a dark stretch of the bank of the Rio Grande.

It's normal around here to see birds flying,
going somewhere, a destination clear in avian mind;
precision and grace is a bright little bluebird
darting and wheeling from limb to limb,
rooftop to headstone to phone line to limb
as the Sun warms the 9 a.m. morning;
grace like sparrows rising in curving,
determined arcs from one home to another
without error, without fail.

Keep your eye on the sparrow.

Twenty-two days into the new year,
shots fired during a fight
in a Dearborn, Michigan school parking lot.

Did you see that robin graze itself just now,
coming out of the tree and falling.
Did you see that happen just then.
He fell so hard. I don't think he's okay.

Thirty-five days into the new year,
a young man with a mind made of trouble
lumbers through the miniature halls of a Florida grade school,
killing two teachers and six child students.

That starling meant to fly to the top
of that tree over there. But did you *see*.
Did you see that he struck something
invisible in the sky. The impact broke his neck.
Did you see that streak of panicking black static.
Did you see the starling fall.

Forty-one days into the rough beast of a new year,
an angry and jobless machinist slouches towards Bethlehem, PA
and automatically opens fire with his automatic gun
on automatic Americans emptying out of the automatic church
on a Sunday morning, nearer my god to thee.

Over there. Did you see that.

That sparrow somehow missed that there was glass there
and flew head first into that office building window.
The impact broke his neck. Did you hear that.
Did you see that sparrow dead on the ground.

Without error, and without fail,
a magpie plummets in a nosedive to its death,
slamming into a patch of icy February sidewalk
in the financial district of Philadelphia,
the City of Brotherly Love.

Asylums Were Made So Nobody Would Have To Leave

The photographer shows me all the pictures he took
of the numerous insane asylums, abandoned and long-defunct,
that he has spent time visiting and photographing
during his travels all across Old Europe and Old America.
Who knew there ever used to be a scary Old America
until these pictures were seen, these sepia tone horrorscapes
of benches with manacles in spider-webbed laboratories
covered in a dusting of ground-up memories and time?
Who could remember that there used to be mansions
where only screams and shouts and chandeliers made their homes,
where the chairs came with strange cones attached to the backs of them,
operating benches in the middle of two-lane bowling alleys
in the middle of laundry rooms in the middle of homemade churches?
Of all the photographs this man shows to me, though,
only one has a voice I can nearly hear and find myself terrified of:
a piano, carved of dark oak with beautifully-sculpted legs
stands alone in a room full of dirt and broken glass and bloodstains,
and underneath the most uncomfortable-looking piano stool I've ever seen
there's torn and faded sheet music lying curled up on the floor
like dove wings clipped, like Christ's wrappings in the cave
and what I would not give to know the final melody of this place.

After Giovanni Bellini's *Christ Blessing,*
c. 1500

In this painting of the Christ, committed
by Giovanni Bellini onto oil and canvas
in one of the very first centuries of history,
we can see clearly the conclusion to all the
cruel punishments and unspeakable agony
that the foretold torturers laid down on the Jesus,
the symbols of divine aspect after the crucifixion
that caused him to lose an awful lot of weight
while at the same time keeping a real tight
and fit tone, with his pale, alabaster white
skin softly reflecting the golds and baby blues
of an early morning Galilee farmland sunrise;
note the sunshine-ray-shaped brass halo
around the head looking all 70's surfer-like;
we can see also Bellini's studious attention
to the details in the soft, gathered fabric
of the purple dress or *toga* or *sarong*
or *whatever that is* that Christ has on
that wraps and covers his slender waist
and shoulders while at the same time
tastefully yet clearly displaying the wounds
and six-pack of the Christ as well as
the stigmata in the palm of his right hand,
rendered in a muted wine colour to effect;
also note the bruises where the soldiers
got him good with a hubcap or something.
We notice that the world around Christ
seems at once sanctified and yet unchanged,
with farmers in the background making their way
through a pasture while in the foreground
we see two little rabbits of two different colours
at furious play as though there wasn't anything
especially marvelous about what is happening
in this moment in time - we also must take note
of the countenance of Christ; a careful observer
will undoubtedly remark on what is plainly visible,
what appears to be a state of high heavenly irritation,
like *what the hell did you do to me, you asswipes*
in the dull pallor behind his blankly staring
and yet really ticked-off brown eyes.
While we can't know what Bellini intended
by this expression on the face of the Christ,
we can guess; we *do* know that once you've forgiven the 77th

sin against you, you've done all that anyone
can really ask of you, and at that point
you can basically just *have at it* and go to town
as far as revenge goes.

Response to Botticelli

What little we know about
Mr. Botticelli, the artist,
paints a very graphic
and depressing picture
of a painter who knew
next to nothing at all about
the ages-old, human practice
of basic, delivery-based childbirth.
The "Birth of Venus"
we remember Botticelli for
reveals a lack of profound care
and research on the artist's part.
Firstly, childbirth takes place
inside of a medical hospital
in a white surgery room
with an operating table,
with doctors and nurses,
with medical instruments,
with stirrups and scalpels;
anyone who was ever born
remembers with vivid vividity
how there are bright lights
in a delivery operating room.
Secondly, people get born
out of the front of women,
not standing on a clamshell.
Thirdly, delivery rooms
do not have ribbon princesses,
or angels that float over you
and blow religious air at you
while you are getting born.
Taken as a whole, it is hard
to take Botticelli seriously.

Seriously.

Tell Me What It Makes You Think About

I spent a day at the museum, where I exhibited no reaction to any of the art on display. There was a giant six-foot-high sculpture constructed of red and orange and yellow crayons, designed to look like a fire frozen in time, and I went right up to it and felt nothing at it. I felt nothing at it intensely, in my bones and through the skin of my arms, until the sculpture's eyes started to betray its emotions, showing me that my intense non-reaction had made it feel ashamed and worthless. There was a small chandelier, fashioned from a cluster of pine cones and orbited by an afro of black wire, lit by a spotlight obviously bought at Home Depot, and I think I was supposed to get a message about courage from this thing, but instead I walked up close and stood under it and folded my arms and gave no reaction to it. As hard as I could. Tears started to drip from the chandelier like wax melting. There was a painting, in mostly muted yellows and blacks depicting two naked witches, a brunette and a redhead, sharing a nighttime broom ride up into Heaven. The artist had been careful to make the two witches differently-shaped, one a bit slender and the other one on the chubby side. You could see how the artist gave some thought as to how naked witch tits would move, or seem to move, while high up in the rare air where you can start to see Heaven approaching. I stood in front of this painting and gave it nothing. The look on my face neither respected nor insulted the work; the look on my face, if you were there and happened to see me, was the look of someone trying to find, in the far-off distance, something meaningful. The witches could not have cared less what I thought of them.

Guess What the Beach Looks Like
(after Picasso's "Bathers with a Toy Boat")

You set out to show us a paradise
in ochre oils, faded, in cerulean dawbs;
your caretaker described for you
what he saw that day on the beach at Menorca:
two buxom women, unashamedly naked
and playing with a toy boat on the sand.

Though celebrated for your vision,
you were obviously born with blindness
and so needed to make your guesses,
estimations of what humans looked like.
And the people called your works *cubist*
as a term of endearment for your struggles.

What was it like to live celebrated
and yet never see the parades in your name,
and yet never know the sting of flashbulbs in your eyes,
and yet never see the nudes who posed before you?

You imagine what limbs, breasts
and heads must look like to sighted people
and you go from there; you make two bathers,
and then you add what you think of in your head
when you hear the words "toy" and "boat".

Your caretaker must have told you
that stormy skies rumble and crack
fearfully in almost green light,
that there was a giant, deformed man
looming above the darkened horizon
and marching through the sea
ominously, silently towards the bathers.

Did you think to ask your caretaker
why there was a giant man standing
at the far, other end of the ocean?
Did you worry that you picked the wrong day
to go to the beach to do some painting?
Did the sunlight feel like moonlight on your face?
Pablo, honey, how much did your lips move
as you asked for the tube of azure oil?

The Thoughts of My Mind When I Look At
Johannes Vermeer's 1658 Painting "The Milkmaid",
Which I Only See Kind of Randomly, But Still

She's taking her sweet time
pouring that milk; I'll tell you what.

Somebody needs to do something
about that wall; it's all chipped and dingedy.

She looks like she's about to slowly
open her eyes and look at me looking at her.

That black intercom above the basket
by the window; it seems out of place.

The bullet holes in the wall behind her
tell me that her neighborhood is bad.

She looks like she's about to slowly
open her eyes, see me there, and smile.

The foot warmer on the floor behind her
looks like an early, baby television set.

In a way that only I can understand,
that window looks very Dutch to me.

She looks like she's about to slowly
open her eyes towards the Dutch window.

There's no way she can be comfortable
wearing that top while milkmaiding.

I'd hate to think that wicker basket
on the wall is full of kittens, but there it is.

She looks like she's about to slowly
open her eyes, see me there, and scream.

V.
Cinnamon Imperial

Music Brings Us Together

Rachmaninoff's Piano Concerto No.4,
and suddenly, the pianist stops playing,
fingers come to a halt, the notes fading quick
like some small scream in a forest cut off abruptly;
his bowtie snaps; he cries out loud for his mother,
yelling it, really, as though his room was on fire;
mother, please, I need you, mother, please
and there's a rumble in the amphitheater,
dresses and tuxedos rise from velvet cushions;
there's a rising hush, a rumbling muttering
and people cannot believe they paid for this
and after a full minute of his screaming
the house lights slowly come up, warming
one by one, yellow stars taking their places
for act one, scene one of the evening sky
and I want to feel bad for him, this pianist,
from all the way up here in this empty balcony,
I really do, but he also happens to be my brother,
and, actually, I miss my mother, too.

The Hailstorm
for Rhiannon, remembered always

I stood beside you
while you held your phone
at arms' length.

On that day, strangely,
the cancer that was wresting you away from me
and over to the other side
in invisible increments of hours and days
was also allowing you one good day,
or at least most of one,
and you loved cloudy skies and
freakish weather.

How you loved them.

It was that afternoon,
as I stood by your side
in the threshold of our front door,
watching you as you watched
and filmed the loud and sudden
hailstorm pounding our doorstep
that I knew I'd have to make peace
with the idea that one bright afternoon,
sometime soon, you would be gone.

I watched as stones of ice
rained down from the hidden sun,
striking up an impromptu bell choir
upon our rusted red mailbox
and the hoods of our cars.

I stood beside you
and I loved that your fascination
seemed to ease your lips into half of a smile
at least for those several minutes.

We both worried about cracks in the glass.

A few days after you died,
I sat with family and friends in a quiet living room
and your best friend cried
when she said that all those years
that pain and sickness had put on your face

were now on mine.

Little dents in the metal.
Tiny cracks in the windshield.

And you're gone.

Take Care of Yourself

You're eating your breakfast
by yourself now, the kids are already on the bus;
this is that time in the morning you usually have to yourself;
the Today show is on the TV in the other room;
you make almost no sound at the table
and you have no idea that I am with you.

You poke with your spoon at the bowl;
the last few frosted cornflakes lily-pad
beneath the surface of the milk;
you look over to the stack of bills
on the messy kitchen counter
and your eyes blink pink carnations into the room;
you have no idea that I am with you.

You finish the cereal
and sip coffee too weak to be of help;
you make steadying motions with your hands
as if to prepare yourself for the act of standing up
but you think twice about going to the window;
you would rather stay seated at the table
than go look outside to see
if today looks like the day I died.

I wish I was still alive.
You have no idea how much I miss you.

Using a Candle to Tell the Time

The face of the clock on the wall
loses its numbers one by one;
it might be the little bit of candlelight
fooling my senses this late but
they fade away before my eyes,
starting with the number twelve
in a clockwise progression
until all the numbers are gone,
and then the minute and second hands
wave a last goodbye to me,
and then all that I can do
is consider where the flame is now
on that candle on the mantel,
think of where that little fire is dancing
as the new midnight for me,
and when there is less of the candle
I'll imagine that as another hour gone
until there are no more hours,
until that place in the Arabian desert
where all our hours come from
is deserted and windy in the moonlight
and it's become pitch dark in here
and how come, *why is it*
that you have not called me yet
to tell me where you are?

Honeycomb

I was able to see into the future after I chomped into that honeycomb,
but first I was found writhing on the ground shouting nonsense
I was never more afraid than I was in that delirium's sweet abyss
the traveling doctor said that my love at last had turned to venom
and that I needed to stay a few nights alone in a distant, healing temple
I was to avoid the sun and moon and be sure to be in bed by nightfall

It was the end of the day, the cold blue start of the evening's nightfall
when I first felt the forbidden, unholy gifts of the flesh of that honeycomb;
I saw myself aged ten years in a silent film playing between my temples
and at first I mistook the vision for the voice of pain or abject nonsense
and then I knew I was wrong, that my veins now carried a venom,
that my mind had become equipped to dip me into a prescient black abyss.

I found I could witness the events to come in the dark smoke of an abyss
the color of mystery and whispered fear, the cricketful hue of nightfall;
I could see myself old and alone because of the blood flow of the venom;
I saw you, too, old and without me because of that cursed honeycomb;
I began to live, breathe and speak the flame-shaped laws of nonsense;
I spent of lot of nights dodging the spotlight of the moon in that temple.

Imagine me running in ragged robes through the stone halls of that temple;
picture me howling like Renfield in the clutches of that groaning abyss;
fathom the terror in my spit dribbling in excitable gobs of silvery nonsense;
the visions of a future I could not prevent always waited until nightfall
to ensnare me in the glue of the nightmare's throbbing honeycomb,
there was madness in the power I'd taken, lunacy in that plasmic venom.

Now I go nowhere. I stay here and drink wine that tastes of black widow venom
and no one ever comes to see me in this hall of screams, this silent temple
where the bread is the same as the fruit is the same as the honeycomb
is the same as the dream is the same as the honey is the same as the abyss
is the same as the morning is the same as each noon is the same as the nightfall
is the same as the song is the same as the creed is the same as the nonsense.

To say we will pay no price for a wish come true is nothing but nonsense;
for biting into that terrible fruit I pay each time my heart pumps venom
into my veins and I stumble, crying after the ghost of you upon each nightfall,
lurching up and down the jagged, frozen stone stairs of this desolate gray temple
hoping to catch up to the memory of you in this everlasting panic, this abyss
that found me the night I uttered a prayer and tore into that honeycomb.

The nonsense psalms fly like invisible sparrows up in the rafters of this temple;
I've saved a glass of venom champagne for you
here in the pitch of this quiet abyss.
Come the moon and stars; come nightfall; come dine
on this honeycomb with me.

ten a.m. is hard

thirteen suns and moons have come and gone
since they said I have the job, background passed.
as far as one knows. ten in the morning has its own
brand of sunshine that lights up the tiles in this kitchen.
the black and white (and cold and dirty) oddfellow floor
glows barely perceptibly, like a déjà vu that stays,
makes the kitchen look just as out of time as me.
we are rarely as sure by the light of morning
about what we were certain of the night before.
the door to the fridge opens by itself, succeeding
in startling. a flock of pale brown birds escapes
and flies through my house until I open the front door
to permit exit. wishing time was not so visible.

Accept What Is Happening

There is a life that contains a galaxy that contains a world that contains a continent that contains a nation that contains a state that contains a city that contains me, and a painting framed in hand-carved gold. This painting is being looked at by me and telling me about a small, red fire in a wooded area of a grey, overcast world that has a lot of Autumn in it. Maybe this painting is actually an open window. In the background in the painting, through some breaks in the trees, an almost blue sky is visible. But it seems so far away, in the perspective of the painting. The sky, seen between the distant trees, seems so far away that nothing can probably be done about this fire. This fire will probably burn until it no longer wants to. There are red leaves on the ground around the fire, but I can't see the fire because it is obscured by pink smoke, which seems to roll in the air slowly, like the ruddy ink breath of an octopus. The smoke is actually coming out of the painting, out into the museum, and I can smell it. This acrid smoke smells like a spicy perfume, a dizzying potpourri, combined with the scent of the first time I ever smelled my mother's lipstick. I suddenly remember the first girl who ever let me touch her. I suddenly remember feeling sad when I learned that my aunt used to be a nun. I suddenly remember that when my mother used to sing to me as a baby, sometimes it sounded like she was crying. Maybe this painting is actually an open window.

To Journey Under Sightless Stars,
To Live Beneath Benighted Heaven

We learn a lot about ourselves when we study the people who aren't alive anymore, the people who used to stand where we stand and eat where we eat, love where we love. We learn a lot about ourselves as human people when we study what the people who used to be alive used to do when money was hard to come by, when it wasn't so rare to beg. We are not hobos now, but we could be, if the right events happened to the world, and so, just in case, we need to learn from the example of the dead. We don't look out for each other, the way humans are supposed to. But hobos did. They did. They had each other's backs. And they left signs behind for their brothers and sisters to read on trees and bridge supports and barns and houses. Little cartoons whispering to you about safety and danger. One of the old hobo signs in America meant to tell you that *this is a place to stay*, and it looked like the astronomical sign for Jupiter. This symbol meant something completely different in England. This was because England and America never really learned to like each other. Except for Princess Di. The sign also meant something completely different to Jupiter, though what it means or meant to Jupiter we'll never know. There's a sign Swedish hobos used to leave behind for other hobos to see, probably scratched into the sides of maroon barns and into the skin of chestnut trees out there that meant *leave this place quickly*, and the sign looked like a rooster. Things were always so different in the United States. In America, a hobo sign that looked like a rooster meant that you would find a rooster in the village. Meanwhile, in downtown Africa, in all of history forever and ever and ever and even up to right now, because of the meanness of the world, one of the hobo signs left on tree trunks by hobos looks like a stick figure with his head in his hands, and it's meant for people who are not hobos, and it means that you have to be careful in this town, because you'll never know if the person you're deciding not to help is actually God.

The Rusted Harvest
for Matt McDonald

They said we could expect frequent lightning,
damaging winds, and golf-ball-sized hail
countywide
until 9:30 tonight.
That's what the woman on the weather said.
My friends and I stand outside on the apartment balcony
and watch the heavy, insistent rain start to pour down,
shining slivers in the day's late gloom,
the rusted harvest colors of dusk darkening
where the stars will be in just a few hours.

Every couple of minutes a beautiful flare
of bright violet or green veins the skies
ferocious
and I can see it in his eyes:
my learned friend Matt looks on the verge of explaining to me
why lightning looks like it goes from here to there,
why it sometimes seems to hang in the air like that,
the temperature, how lightning could burn the sun if it could,
how every five seconds equals a mile to countdown
30 seconds between safety and the tallest tree in the park
but I don't want my stratospheres put to rest with explanations and theories.

See, all these theories and theses you want quote to me, my friend,
they only serve to cage that bird in my head,
the little cuckoo bird who likes to take fancy flights
where lightning strikes and other "natural phenomena" are concerned
and that's why I tell you *ssssshhhhhhhhhhhhh I don't want to know*
and I know you say you think it's beautiful that mankind has nearly completely
decoded the secret recipe for fire in the sky
and I can respect where you're coming from even though I've never been there
but tonight is one of those nights to learn again
how beauty lives or dies by the eyes that see it
because, in my life, every time I learned some new fact or other about the world
I got burned, I got burned in the sense that another of the universe's mysteries
dies
every time I turn to page 60; when I was young my quest for knowledge
was my pain, my thirst to know the heaven of that first kiss
but with the bliss of leaping over that precipice
came lessons 2) tears win arguments,
and 3) if chocolate appears in the house all of sudden,
go make yourself busy elsewhere
see, knowing the biology of lightning

it isn't worth it, to me, I love my wonder too much,
even as a child with tears in my eyes afraid of it,
shrinking behind my father in the yard I loved it
in the same crazy way we love a roller-coaster's gift of nausea,
the way we frown upon talking out loud about déjà vu
see, the harder I work at forgetting 8th grade science lessons
about thunderstorms,
the sooner I can come up with my own reasons and explanations for lightning,
explanations I can guarantee will be a lot cooler than
supercooling, superheating and charge separations—
as a matter of fact, did you know that bolts of lightning
are really just neon anger lines emanating from the heads
of giant, invisible and furious ghosts in the sky?
That's a comfort to me, and I hope it is for you, too.
Tomorrow night, I plan on flying a kite
in the thunderstorm I've heard we can expect,
and I can only hope that when the weather's rage gives way to silent
constellations,
when I pull that kite back down to earth,
I hope I'll find that someone up there has attached a note for me to read,
a wrinkled slip of paper scorched and clinging to my line
bearing, in the child-like scribble of a god,
a simple, three-word command,
"cut it out".

Amare

I found a stray wish
on my doorstep last night;
its breathing was ragged
and it looked terrible,
fur all matted and soaked
through by the cold rain,
emaciated and scared;
it mewed weakly at me
and I wondered to myself
if this was an abused wish,
if this wish had run away
from a heart that didn't love it;
it looked like it was afraid
to let itself trust me
as I reached down to pick it up;
it fluttered in a panic in my arms
as I carried it home
cooing to it softly, shushing it gently
and I wondered if I was wrong,
that perhaps this wish was not abused
but *abandoned*
and didn't know a soul
never knew a soul
and then I realized
that I wanted it to know me
and to trust me to love it
like no one ever had before,
so when I got home
I fed the wish some soup
and some good meat kibbles
and then I gave this wish a bath
until its coat was shiny and pink again
and then I let the wish lay down
on some quilts by the fireplace.
I let this wish catch its breath
and fall asleep through the night,
feeling safe and feeling as though
there was someone in this world
who loved it very much,
someone in this world
who it could love back
and think of as *home*
if it ever wanted to.

Today, the wish spent every hour
by my side, purring and all aglow,
until the afternoon darkened
into the first long minutes of night,
until the time came
for it to fly away
to become what it was meant to be
and to accomplish what it was meant to do
and I tried to be strong;
it never did see my tears
as it looked at me
from the cradle of my open palm;
I nodded to it,
told it to be free
told it to remember where I was
and that it could come see me
any time it wanted to
and then I heard it mew
and then it flew,
leaving my hands
light as a feather
and I looked up
just as the raindrops
started to tap and ring
on the ground all around me;
the wish was flying up
and getting smaller and smaller,
away and away
like a little pink kite
jellyfishing its way
softly, up and up and up
into the syncopating,
violet meadow
of a night-time sky
in a storm.

A Kindhearted Woman Lives Here

Even if you were not simply *poor*,
even if you were something somehow worse than poor,
there is a woman in that house you see there
who would, smilingly, take you in for a few nights
out of the plain American goodness of her heart;
walk, trudge along, walk towards her safety
before the deputized Sun awakens and sees you;
even if you have murder in the years behind you,
even if you have bodies and the screams of broken bottles
and a car left idling on a pier somewhere,
even if the police really wanted to know where you were
she would only ask that you take none of the lives under her roof;
you see how small her ramshackle is, there by that clearing in the woods,
barely bigger than a shack, no weathervane, barely anything at all
inside that black and brown and ashen clapboard pastiche;
go on, get yourself to the front door of her gift box;
know that if you were to confess your double life as a werewolf
in borrowed pants and stolen suspenders
she would only ask that when the Moon is up and shining
you keep those shades all the way drawn down
in that extra room she'll have for you in the back;
don't steal anymore, don't steal from her modest collection of dolls,
don't steal, and be nothing but kind to the cats she keeps around her home;
look now, one of the many cats of the premises, he's lying there like symbolism,
a big orange cat, he's lying in the weeds in front of her home;
he's looking you up and down and deciding that he does not see you;
the flame on the candle in her window flickers like a thought almost spoken
and for a moment you think you remember what color Christmas was;
for a moment you remember the dream about there being no more work,
the dream about leaping out of the blue window, the copper penny dream,
the dream where you had a thousand conversations with the wind
by the side of a road where none of the riders could see you.
When was the last time you went to sleep without starting a fire first?
When was the last time you had some soup, something good
that wasn't the rain and the grass in your cupped hands?
When was the last time you had some bread that was not dead?
When do you think the dream should come to an end
and why are you standing still, what are you waiting for?
Walk up the steps and over the gray cat that sees you with her eyes closed;
let the stone of worry fall from your palm and knock on the door.
A kindhearted woman lives here.

In Memory of My Neighbor, Carol,
Who Has Not Died Yet

I will probably always remember you
as the woman with the pink winter coat
that I never talked to except for maybe once
to ask you if you knew anything about the power outage
that one night, that one august, the one time,
and that might not have even been you, actually,
but even if that wasn't you that night
I'll always cherish my maybe incorrect memory of you;
I will mostly likely always remember you
as not really having a face at all,
since I couldn't see your face from my window
as you pulled out of your driveway
every morning to go off to work;
it's possible I might even let myself cry
at some point in the future
if it should happen to occur to me
that all this time I've just been assuming
that your name is really Carol.

Did You Mean…?

I launch Chrome from my desktop; Google is my home page.
We're going to a party tonight, and we're supposed to bring a salad,
so I'm searching for unique ways to make or change up
a Caesar's salad for at least six
and Google asks me upon my first inquiry *did you mean Julius Caesar?*
No, Google, I didn't mean Julius Caesar; I'd have asked you about Julius Caesar
if I wanted to know about Julius Caesar. *Et tu, Google*?

Google is convenient though, like opportune rain, or that phone call
on your cell that can free you from a face-to-face conversation
you're looking not to have with that person you were hoping not to run into,
but the fact that we have all just passively accepted the existence and proliferation
of artificial intelligence means, of course, that we have had to trade off
some of our sense of normality for the ability to go online
and look for the things we may or may not want to find.

I'm scared, and I'm not afraid to say so.

I'm scared that every time I search for something on Google
the first results are not really *results* but more and more questions:
Did you mean Marcus Aurelius? Did you mean typhoid fever?
Did you know that someone is skulking around in your back yard even as we speak?
Did you mean to look as frightened as you look right now?
People who chose to feel the same fear that you are feeling in this moment
also chose to feel anxiety, panic and terror.

Every day, I find some brand new proof for the non-existence of God,
some kidnapped girls locked in a basement for forty years,
legislation that makes friendly fire not only legal but mandatory,
dance crazes that sweep the nation under a wave of stupidity
but every day when I sit down at my computer at work,
it's all *yeah, well, people who chose to doubt the existence of God*
also chose to go golfing, also chose a Vegan diet, also chose to go on a killing spree;
people who chose to feel weird about the thought that there is something greater than us
out there in the Moonless night sky, up among those barely audible stars
also chose to let themselves feel depressed once in a while;
some people also chose to *fear their mirror;* some people also chose to just *feel*.

I wanted to find out about the X-Men,
but I didn't want to find out about X-rated men.

Or maybe I *did,* but I didn't know it but Google did and isn't that interesting?
I wanted to find out more about X-rated women,
but I didn't want to find out about my exes
and what their lives have turned into and isn't that a shame?
I wanted to find out more about the day I am going to die,
so I made a deal with myself: every day, I'd go onto Google to ask it
if I would ever see my mother and father again,
if there actually *was* a Heaven, if religion and faith were really worth it
and not just nonsense, and I would check back every day
to see if Google would answer me in a different way.

I type *I'm scared* into the search field.

Did you mean to ask why are we here?
Did you mean God, or were you looking for something else?
Did you mean to be crying right now?

Early Messengers

As the sunlight of the morning's dawn
bursts through the slats of my bedroom's
window's white plastic shade
I blink my eyes uncontrollably;
the light of a new day is so terribly strong.
The light of the morning part of a new day
after a last night of revelry is very strong, also.
As my eyes flutter back into place,
the autumn chill finds its autumnly way
into my bones as I scamper out of bed
in only half of my PJ's and up onto my feet.
Wearing only one half of a pajama,
I stumble to the window and open the shade a crack
to see the birds that are around in the morning
flying away in a direction that I can only call South.
What do these birds mean, flying so early
and rudely past my house at this hour?
Are these birds messengers, come to tell me
that harbinger birds are on their way?
And if so, why are these messenger birds even necessary?
Wouldn't the harbinger birds be enough?

The Day He Decides to Leave

Eleven in the morning is the last hour he has before the Sun really begins to burn. This is the largest, brightest thought cometing through the hornet buzz universe of his mind. For so long he's watched how the people do it, how they move their bodies, how they rise with a cry and fall with a laugh and leap and jump. Though he only has hay and feathers for brains, he has finally reasoned all of it out and he is done with the years of agony coursing through the straw of him. You know him; he is empty but still has a soul and that soul has come to a place where he knows that he cannot live one minute longer like this and his face is the face of every epiphany you've ever seen. See the fabric of his face crease with determination. See him strain to reach behind and lift himself off the stake in his back. See him do it. See him win and land roughly on the ground. See him reaching down, brushing himself off. See him tilt his head back, craning the potato-sack burlap of his neck, squinting his black magic marker X's up into the sky, hoping, thinking, following the flight of a large, dark bird. See him look this way and that; see him search for any people around. See him come to know he is alone. See him break into a run; see the tears drying on the yellowed cloth of his face in the wind. See his floppy gray hat fly off his crooked head as he runs as fast as he can through the corn, running through the green and gold to the heat lines of the horizon, to the beginning and the ending of the world.

Come and Be Astounded

Production is what they call it
when a magician *produces* something
from completely out of nowhere,
like a bright, frightened rabbit
out of a worried construction helmet,
or a dove from a cage full of crows,
or even some smoke from a fire.
One of the black things about magic,
one of the things I fear the most
is that I will attend a performance
and before I know it, the magician
will produce my mother, who has been dead
for a number of years, and make her appear onstage.
Then he will make her look at me and speak.
Then, he will make me talk to her.

They like to say the word *vanish*
when a magician forces a thing to be gone,
like a tiger, say, or a pretty lady in glittery underwear,
or a very old sin, still writhing, committed long ago
and still hissing in its painted basket
shivering inside of a Bedouin tent
in a desert located behind the poker face
of a very careful person, a silent and quiet
audience member just like myself.
Magicians also have a perverse thing
for transformation; they like to make milk become blood;
turn a loud, spoiled brat into a gasping canary,
an audience member's money into their own.
This is why it's so important to always be yourself;
there are professionals out there who endeavor
to make you something you are not.

And heaven forbid a magician
should ever forget what it takes
to set me back down to familiar Earth
after floating me in the air for a while;
that's why I don't go to those shows.
How lovely it would be if magicians could teach us
how to get ourselves out from underneath
the blood-stained padlock of overdue bills;
how lovely it would be if magicians knew
how to instantly move silos of gold to Ethiopia;
how lovely it would be if magicians knew

more practical intentions for their skills;
sawing a woman in half is all fine and good,
but we can and should demand more from them:
show us not simply how a heart can be broken,
but how it can be put back together again.

For Lucifer, On the Occasion of Your Banishment
after Ricardo Bellver's "El Angel Caído"

Your wings are as beautiful
as any angel's I have ever seen before,
though yours are made of stone now.

I shouldn't look long at you,
for fear some sympathy may grow
in my chest for you, for your pain.

Serpents chain you to the Earth
by wrapping themselves around your legs
and curling their tails to tree trunk and heavy stone,
their hisses replacing the kisses to your forehead
that your golden father once gave you
when you were good, and obedient.

I should not behold your permanent crisis;
I should walk along past you, toward the rose garden,
and let the flowers' scents and setting suns
take me to a dream.

To see you like this hurts me.
You live this moment of banishment
over and over forever, brows bent in shock,
your lips burst open in such a way
it appears as though you are frozen
in the middle of asking your father "why?"

Perhaps he heard your question,
and you were given your answer.

Scalpel. Sponge. Forceps.

Help me hold this angel down,
you will notice that his wings are beating
back very rapidly against the operating bench,
almost as though he is aware that
he will not live through this procedure.
One almost regrets that this is necessary.

Pay close attention to his lips and eyes
as we work together; watch for dilation
and rapid movement. We will start
with an injection of a strong anesthetic,
something to put this angel to sleep.

The first thing I am going to need
is the bone rasp. Hand that to me.
Next, let me have the cartilage crusher.
Quickly, now. I'll need a sponge here, please.
Removing the angel's ability to fly
is, of course, our first priority.

Arugula

Arugula is a giant monster that lives most of his life
in the beautiful, amazing and horrible country of Japan.
Sometimes he flies or swims to other countries
like America, or Rio de Janeiro, where he breaks things there also.
But mostly, Arugula attacks the innocent and friendly Tokyo people,
unless he is protecting them from another monster, which happens sometimes.
He is very large; he is mountain-sized; that's why he's giant.
Many scientists truly believe, if they don't want to make me mad,
that the giant monster Arugula is a miracle of science because
he has the ears of an elephant, the body of a rat,
the wings of a dragonfly and the arms of a Russian ballet person.
He also has owl eyes, very angry owl eyes, the eyes of an owl
that has had enough of listening to peoples' nonsense.
Arugula doesn't like it when people don't listen to me.
When I tell them to, some scientists think
that Arugula was created when an atom bomb was tested
near a zoo in Russia that had a rat and dragonfly infestation problem.
Still other people, like shaman religious cultural scholar people,
if they don't want another incident where I get really angry,
often say that Arugula, the giant monster, is the living manifestation
of the Earth's desire to punish us for polluting it with our pollution.
People in the sciences and people in the cultures and religions
should get together and agree about Arugula, the giant monster,
and they should get together and make people say yes that Arugula exists,
and people should just listen when they're told about real giant monsters
and not laugh or make faces like they think there's something wrong with me.
People should just listen and not look at me or say anything negative
when they are told about giant monsters that are really real.
People should not be so quick to say that there's no such thing as a monster.
People can be in trouble if they don't believe in giant monsters.
People can upset me, and they shouldn't do that.
People should be afraid of being in trouble.

Come At Me, Bro

The Devil gets locked out of Hell
and panics, struggling with the overwrought iron gates
like an idiot but they won't budge, locked, a firmly hard stone
and it occurs to the Prince of Darkness
that he's going to have to find a new realm to rule

and so up he floats

up through the millions and millions of miles
of dark, lightless, sulfurous underground Earth,
rising, rising, rising and holding his breath,
pinching his nose with forefinger and thumb
so that he doesn't get the bends
as he rises toward the light

and just as his head pokes out of the ground,
I lift my sandaled foot up and then down onto his horny head,
and I stomp him back down under the ground,
underneath the dew-dropped, morning dawn,
big grassy lawn of the world.

I'm Jesus Christ, *bitch*.

Nobody gets past me.

Riviera Dawn

Fuck home, muttered Dorothy,
I'm not clicking my heels
just to go back to that Podunk wasteland.

There's no place like Paris, Dorothy said.
There's no place like Paris, said Dorothy again.
There's no place like Paris, said Dorothy,
over and over again
until everyone around her got blurry
and she could hear harp strings blooming.
And then Dorothy was in Paris.

And then Dorothy was sipping some wine
at a table along the Rue de L'École
de L'Ésperance de L'Ésprit de L'Autre.
And then Dorothy wore a peacock mask
and a tight black lacy bustier
at a pleasure carnival in French woods.
And then Dorothy heard calliope music
and couldn't stop the Ferris Wheels
in her eyes from spinning
even when she closed her eyes.
And then Dorothy never woke up again.

And then a white wooden rocking chair,
on a windy, overcast Riviera dawn,
rocking by itself, on and on.

What Happens When I Invent Her

Whenever I catch myself inventing her
there she is, out of the corner of my eye;
there she is again, recreating me in time
with the music of my own design.

When I close my eyes
to make *her* eyes up from scratch,
imagining them in impossible blues,
forest greens and shadow-striped golds;
she is real the moment I realize
she has replaced my eyes
with the lenses of kaleidoscopes:
the Moon is a crystal ball over the tilting ocean;
the meadows are carpeted in shivering silver blades of grass;
every drop of rain is a different color in this thunderstorm;
this is what happens when I invent her.

I fetish her fingers with my mind;
it isn't hard to do but neither is it easy;
they are graceful, soft and slender
and my fingers curl absently,
almost feeling her fingers laced with mine
until I notice that she has left me,
left me reaching for ladder rungs made of smoke,
climbing on a rope made of pouring rain,
and pushing against the weight of my own words;
this is what happens when I invent her.

When I make her younger than me
it's only to wind up waiting in a rocking chair
outside of a nursery full of newborn stars,
when I make her older than me
it's only to lose sight of her in a crowd dispersing;
she eludes me like a name, like odd logic;
and when I compose the feel of her hair
with my thoughts, her braids dissolve
in the solution of my useless tears;
I fashion her legs from paintings
and dreams and the limbs of young trees
and while I do so she has fixed me to the Earth,
fixed it so I have never taken a step before,
taken every moment I have ever been in "mid-leap"
and chained them together, in reverse,
until I find myself falling so fast and hard

I pass myself on the way down;
this is what happens when I invent her.

Sometimes, in the Winter, I see footsteps impressing themselves
into the snow at night and the thought that I could be right
about angels fills me with terror and hope at the same time;
every once in a while, in the Fall, I'll see the leaves
swirling of their own accord, on an afternoon with no wind to speak of
and I'll have to catch my breath if I don't want it to be taken from me.

Whenever I catch myself inventing her,
all I'm doing is telling a tired joke to a quiet audience at the graveyard,
arrogant enough to think my little fire on the beach will impress the Sun;
I am not fooling anyone; least of all, her.

Is That Joe?

We're getting confirmations at this time of a report that says that the man who for the last hour has been scaling the Statue of Liberty as police look on helplessly is *Joe Mariano*, a construction worker and poet from Bridgeton, New Jersey. Sketches are detailed at this time, but relatives tell our sources that Mariano was recently laid off from his construction job, a position he held for ten years. His father tells our sources that he never heard Joe ever talk about doing something like this. His mother was quoted by another network as saying that she didn't know that he wrote poetry or owned climbing equipment. Mariano's brother, Michael, tells our sources that Joe *did* seem troubled lately, and had difficulty expressing himself except in the form of poetry; Michael also says that Joe had confided to him recently that, quote, "America needs a reboot; something is really wrong with all of us" and that "there isn't a lot of time left."

Inclemency

The strong winds and the piercing rains
knocked out the servers at the newspaper last night.
The news, as a consequence, got to the outside world
a little too late for it to still be considered the news.
The outside world already knew that the Japanese
had almost been earthquaked off the map
before the last of the newspaper bundles
had been dropped off on the sidewalks in the dark,
like latecomers arriving to a house party
when almost everyone's gone and the dip bowl is empty.
The strong winds and the piercing rains
took down a whole slew of telephone poles last night,
and the telephone poles spat out a little bit of lightning
as they crashed onto the roofs of cars under last night's
bright and loud and dark and frightening evening sky.
The strong, powerful winds and the piercing, shrieking rains
flooded the homes of a million ants in town last night.
A million ants evacuated, tried desperately to gather up
everything they owned before the flood came last night.
The strong, howlful winds and the piercing, banshee rains
made it very hard to see what all was going on
outside our windows, on our lawns last night.
Anything could have been happening out there
outside our windows, on our lawns last night
but the blue, piercing winds and strong, jet-black rains
just would not let us see what was happening.
Anything could have been happening out there
in the driving, strong winds and freezing, piercing rains.
What if a man was stuck out there in all of that
and no one gave him shelter because no one could see him?
What if a man was stuck out there in all of that
and no one gave him shelter even though he could be seen?
Would we all be accomplices to whatever happened to him?
Why didn't someone, anyone, anyone of us human beings
go out there in the deathly, freezing winds and the dark, driving rains
to grab him by the arm and pull him into the house where it was warm?
Why didn't we hurry, hurry him to the front porch
where the light bulb swung over the rocking chair
like a hanged man under a tree in a storm?
What in the hell is wrong with us?

The Hush

A rain of cherry blossom petals fell from the sky
that afternoon, in silence, for an hour,
heralded by a single peal of distant thunder
from beyond the mountains.

Every place where the pink petal rains fell
fell silent. The people walked slowly and carefully
all of a sudden, stunned into wordlessness.

The blossom petals fell on our heads,
and covered our windshields, and buried our rooftops,
and obscured our streets and roads and lanes, too;
we looked up into the sky and saw so much pink
there was nothing but the strange emotion
that comes from beholding so much everything
in the bright and rosy quietude.

For that hour, there came no sound between the skyscrapers;
the zoos, the parks, the woods all lost their voices
and the highways, for once, stopped screaming.
Everyone tried to talk but no one could say a word;
I mean, we wanted to speak but we did not know how
with all of this frightening beauty coming down on us.

I tried to find you in that peaceful tempest,
but I couldn't when it grew stronger;
I didn't worry about you though,
because I knew you were also in this storm
and it would be like we were in the same dream.

When we finally did see each other,
the next morning, under a sky full of whispering stars,
all of the things that we wanted to say
just fell away from our minds like ice melting,
like bank notes falling from an airplane,
the echoing ring of an unstruck bell.

Telephone Numbers Die in Los Angeles

If you try to use your cellphone in Los Angeles,
you will become really lost and alone,
because there is something about Los Angeles
that causes cell phones to suddenly be run
and controlled by strange companies;
there is something in the sky that's in the air
in Los Angeles that contributes to the sound of fear
and to mysterious aircraft hovering
just inside of the city-lit clouds at night
and when you look at the little screen on your phone
you'll find that you don't recognize any of the numbers
and the numbers that you thought you had memorized
are not in your phone anymore; you can't find them
and now you can't remember phone numbers
that you need to always be able to remember:
the numbers of your last two significant others,
the number that will actually connect you,
even at midnight, to a real human being
at the bank where all your money lives,
the numbers to all of the people
you like to think of as friends
even though you rarely ever call them,
which is a shame, a damned shame
since they've been sitting there wondering
what's been going on with you lately,
the number your father said you could call
anytime you ever needed anything
and the number to the only hospital in the world
that really knows what's wrong with you;
if you ever go to Los Angeles, please pray first
and tell everyone that you love
that you love them before you go,
just in case Lost Angeles is the kind of place
you could never come home from;
better to leave your phone at home
than take it with you to the city of lost angels.

If We Get Disconnected

The cataclysm will come, and the hospitals and skyscrapers will lose their balance
and stumble, stone giants lethally crumbling over all of us as we run;
we'll be running and then we'll stop running and then we'll run some more
and the sky will go from light blue to a rough, charcoal black in seconds;

we all will yell and scream as the telephone poles become electric slingshots
and a rainstorm of broken glass shatters us from all sides, all hands-on deck
and the sick, orange sky will seem to come loose from its moorings unseen
and dance like a drunk on a very dizzy kitchen floor;

we will run in all directions looking for structures standing still enough
for us to stand beneath as all the main streets and entire front yards and highways
fly up into the rosy air like they forgot about gravity and their role as the ground,
and the world starts to feel like a giant supermarket and we are lost and *where is our mommy?*

Every time we get close to a carport or garage or a house with its front door open,
a piece of airliner or a swimming pool or half of a transit bus crashes down
onto what we were hoping would be safety under a sky turning hurricane green,
and we have to stop on a melting dime and run faster than our screams;

one of us will remain human enough to stop and pick up the screaming baby
that will be sitting in the middle of the blood-soaked road and crying for help;
hopefully, one of us will remain human enough to do that, to help that child
as the Sun suddenly grows so massive that it becomes the sky itself;

I will probably try to call you first to find out where you are
and then tell you that if we get disconnected I love you;

we'd best prepare for that time now; we'd better start honestly practicing
the art of running and crying and praying all at once, one shoe on, one shoe off;
we'd better get good at dialing emergency contacts while upside-down
and we'd better decide right now what sound or bell will tell us in no uncertain terms
here it comes; here comes the cataclysm; here it comes.

The Moon is a Westinghouse Production

We got started late, but the afternoon's quiet hike out at the sleeping volcanoes was only a handful of songs up the highway, quite the lovely drive. It took an eternity but it also seemed to take only a few hours to reach the top of the tallest hill. Took more than forever in breaths when we got there for sure. By the end that we reached, the Sun had been all over the sky, and it had had enough. We noticed the Sun had gone down at some point, but did not remark on it. We noticed that the ground under our shoes changed in some way, but did not remark on it. First crumbling sand, then solid rock, then more crumbling sand, like what's found at the beach. At the crest, after a moment of looking around and rubbing our eyes we realized that night had come. That was moonlight, that shine on the rocks. But why was that light so bright? Because we'd climbed higher than the top of the hill and didn't know so, because the Moon was only ten feet above us by the end. Because we learned the secret that the Moon doesn't reflect light at all, that the Moon actually gives off light, a chalky white luminescence you can feel. Because the Moon, it turned out, was made by Westinghouse; it bore the logo on the side, that area that the world always thought was the Man in the Moon. The surface of the Moon was cloudy and translucent; we could see a massive light bulb inside there. Why was I so quiet? Because I knew saying anything at that moment would have snapped the delicate filament, that moment owned only by us. Why did we have to leave and come back down? Because to let ourselves get pulled away into the night by the Moon would have meant giving up all we knew. Actually, let's not make the same mistake next time we're there. Let's let it happen next time.

Day Glo

It's when I see the Tide detergent logo and I'm in the supermarket variety store and I'm in my mind I think about how the world is going to begin to end, the bright flash in the sky. And I know the world will end in a ball of fire that will look a LOT like kind of like exactly like the Tide detergent logo. I walk past the frozen foods, beyond the floral department, through the school supplies aisle and I *float float float* towards the cleaners and detergents. Where they live. Where they can be bought. And I behold the very small, very tiny and scarce millions and millions of different boxes of detergent powders, powerful in their amber and cadmium cardboard boxes, which shiver on shelves made of metal in rows that are parallel, even, and level even. And I see the Tide. I see the Tide logo, and the Tide detergent logo throbs with the heat of its color right in front of me, the clever design of the logo works most effectively on me, and I suddenly feel the weight of the realization that the world would be a much cleaner place if we were all gone.

To All the Souls Gliding Slowly and Pearlescently
Up to Heaven Who, At the Moment of Total Incineration
At Ground Zero of The First Nuclear Strike in The Final World War,
Just So Happened to Be Purchasing Sex Toys at The Time

Just think of it,
what's happened,
and try to think of it as just.
You could be trying that on,
or *in*, or *out*, forever and ever;
you could be trying to relax
while it goes in all the way for all eternity.
The sound of your voice inquiring
after the kinds of batteries it takes,
the voice of your sound asking
if water will do damage to it,
asking if it will do damage to you
or to someone or something else,
the shocked look on the clerk's face,
the bored look on the clerk's face,
the annoyed clerk, disinterested clerk,
clerk getting very little
in the way of a commission at all,
the clerk thinking thoughts of you
she'd never have thought if you and she
walked past each other ever anywhere else in time,
the cloying cleanser smell throughout the store:
everything has a reason and a purpose, yes, Ecclesiastes?
Yes, these will be your last memories
of your earthbound life, not the coffee you had
before heading out of the house
on the beautiful Spring morning of Doomsday,
not the kiss on the cheek from him or her or x
as you head out the door to go get some,
not the car horns or the giggling babies in radio ads
or that always mailman fellow so robotic,
squat scuttling like a white ladybug
describing in a so slow circle
the curve of the cul-de-sac you live in
as to you he brings never-ending
grocery circulars and utility bills.
And now as you slowly rise up past 25,000 feet
with exactly 75,000 more feet to go before
you arrive at the Pearly Gates,
and as you try to remember the secret knock,
look down at your hands; look down at your waists;

your posture is still in the moment just before the blast;
see that you're still hefting that brutal, black dildo,
evaluating its impressive weight and shine;
see how you still have that vicious strap-on on
over your pants because you couldn't wait to see
how it looked right there at the sales counter;
see the plug's pink sapphire gem twinkling,
the brilliance and color fading to dark
in the ghostly palm of your hand
as you rise further and further
away from daylight's
last hurrah

Rich Boucher, born with HDTV in Woonsocket, Rhode Island, is a laborer, lover, and poet. A page and stage writer with memberships in five national poetry slam teams to his credit (Worcester, Massachusetts in 1995 and 1996, Washington, D.C. in 2001, Wilmington, Delaware in 2007 and Albuquerque, New Mexico in 2008 and 2014), Rich has published four chapbooks of poems and hosted an open reading and slam in Newark, Delaware for several years. Since moving to Albuquerque in March of 2008, Rich has been performing and writing steadily in the Duke City, as well as appearing in several local schools as a guest performer and educator. In 2012, Rich was named to the first inaugural Albuquerque Poet Laureate Selection Committee for a two-year term, and his participation helped to select the City of Albuquerque's first official Poet Laureate. Rich's poems have appeared in numerous literary journals, both in print and online. In January of 2012, Rich appeared as a long-distance guest on the album, "Dylan – Philadelphia Pays Tribute to a Legend", an album featuring various Philadelphia artists performing covers of Dylan songs to benefit Amnesty International and the End Hunger Network; Rich's contribution to the album was a spoken-word rendition of Bob Dylan's "My Back Pages". From the summer of 2016 to the spring of 2017, he served as the Associate Editor and Weekly Poem Curator at Elbow Room Magazine. Rich adds new and unpublished work in audio format from time to time on his bandcamp page at richboucher.bandcamp.com. He lives in Albuquerque, New Mexico with his love Leann and their sweet cat Callie.

Made in the USA
Columbia, SC
14 March 2019